Unleashing Innovation

Unleashing Innovation

How Whirlpool Transformed an Industry

Nancy Tennant Snyder and
Deborah L. Duarte

JOSSEY-BASS
A Wiley Imprint
www.josseybass.com

Published by Jossey-Bass
A Wiley Imprint
989 Market Street, San Francisco, CA 94103-1741—www.josseybass.com

Readers should be aware that Internet Web sites offered as citations and/or sources for further information may have changed or disappeared between the time this was written and when it is read.

Limit of Liability/Disclaimer of Warranty: While the publisher and author have used their best efforts in preparing this book, they make no representations or warranties with respect to the accuracy or completeness of the contents of this book and specifically disclaim any implied warranties of merchantability or fitness for a particular purpose. No warranty may be created or extended by sales representatives or written sales materials. The advice and strategies contained herein may not be suitable for your situation. You should consult with a professional where appropriate. Neither the publisher nor author shall be liable for any loss of profit or any other commercial damages, including but not limited to special, incidental, consequential, or other damages.

Jossey-Bass books and products are available through most bookstores. To contact Jossey-Bass directly call our Customer Care Department within the U.S. at 800-956-7739, outside the U.S. at 317-572-3986, or fax 317-572-4002.

Jossey-Bass also publishes its books in a variety of electronic formats. Some content that appears in print may not be available in electronic books.

The following trademarks are owned by Whirlpool Corporation or its related companies: Whirlpool, KitchenAid, Maytag, Jenn-Air, Amana, Brastemp, Consul, Bauknecht, Gladiator, Eco-House, Duet, Inspired Chef, Gatorpak, and Centralpark. All other trademarks are owned by their respective companies.

Blu-Ray Disc™ is a registered trademark of Sony Kabushiki Kaisha Corporation. All rights reserved. XBox™ is a registered trademark of Microsoft Corporation. All rights reserved. iPod™ is a registered trademark of Apple Computer, Inc. All rights reserved.

Library of Congress Cataloging-in-Publication Data

Snyder, Nancy Tennant, date.
  Unleashing innovation : how Whirlpool transformed an industry / Nancy Tennant Snyder and Deborah L. Duarte.
    p.   cm.
  Includes bibliographical references and index.
  ISBN 978-0-470-19240-5 (cloth : alk. paper)
    1. Whirlpool Corporation—Management.   2. Washing machine industry—Technological innovations—United States—History.   3. Household appliances industry—Technological innovations—United States—History.   I. Duarte, Deborah L., date.   II. Title.
  HD9971.5.W374W457   2008
  338.7'68388—dc22

                                                                    2008016484

Printed in the United States of America
FIRST EDITION
HB Printing   10 9 8 7 6 5 4 3 2 1

Contents

Foreword

In the late 1990s, Whirlpool Corporation was facing a defining moment. Our company was almost ninety years old and had faced defining moments four or five times during our history. Over this period, the company had gone from being a one-product, one-customer manufacturer of washing machines to being the global leader of marketing and manufacturing major household appliances, with revenues over $10 billion. We sold its products in over 170 different markets, and the Whirlpool brand was the top-selling appliance brand in the world.

In 1997, we rolled out our "post-globalization" strategy, which we called our Brand-Focused Value-Creation strategy. The strategy was (and is) quite straightforward. To succeed and create value in the global appliance business, we must perform well in three areas: (1) global operating platform . . . cost, quality, and asset utilization; (2) trade customers . . . alignment, service, B-T-B; and (3) strong brand loyalty . . . great brands and winning repeat purchases from our consumers.

In many respects this strategy reflected our evolution from a manufacturer to a great trade sales organization and a now to consumer-driven brand company. Our strong belief was that success in all three areas would lead to above-average growth and value creation.

By 1999 it was clear to us at Whirlpool that there was something critical missing in our strategy. Growth rates were flat, average selling prices were going down, and margins had become a cost game. We somewhat reluctantly concluded after deep soul searching that the "something" was innovation. In 1999, we were not an innovative company; we were only an "operating" company. To succeed and to execute our Brand-Focused Value-Creation strategy, we concluded we had to be both innovative and operationally excellent.

Nancy's recap of our innovation journey is well documented in this book. She describes very vividly the learning process that we've gone through in trying to embed innovation throughout our company. In 1999, we certainly had no idea how to do this, or the path that it would take. We did know, however, that we would take a principles-based all-inclusive approach in building innovation as a core competency across our entire company. Nancy captures the steps that we took along the way, the learnings, the successes and setbacks. Looking back ten years later, we are embedding innovation across our company; it is a critical business process that we must continually improve. Persistence and perseverance have proven to be the important leadership characteristics that have enabled our success to date.

I believe this book will provide some refreshing insights to others who are serious about building an innovative organization. This is not a how-to book; there are plenty of those already. This book offers examples of the struggle that organizations and leadership groups will likely experience with a large-scale innovation transformation. It also offers some great learnings and tools that can shorten the implementation time by allowing organizations to learn from others' experience.

Overall, the book is a "real-life" example of how innovation can transform an organization and is a great read for anyone serious about making innovation a reality in his or her organization.

Jeff M. *Fettig*
Chairman and CEO
Whirlpool Corporation

Preface

We wrote this book to contribute to the new and growing field of inclusive innovation—innovation from everyone and everywhere—in large organizations. When we started this approach to innovation at Whirlpool Corporation in 1999, very few companies were on this path. Today Whirlpool has become a teacher of sorts; many companies come to benchmark us to understand both how we got started and where we are today. Many world-class companies now share our path.

The Whirlpool story is both unique and compelling. Whirlpool is one of the few companies in the world that have transformed every aspect of their business to drive continuous innovation. Whirlpool has differentiated itself in innovation by creating a sustainable and repeatable innovation model and by embedding it in every aspect of the organization: vision, mission, strategy, operations reviews, design, communications, reward, education, career paths, financials, and more. What makes Whirlpool unique is that it has chosen a path that shuns the popular notion that innovation can come only from the geniuses at the top. Whirlpool "innovated innovation" by putting systems and processes in place that enable every person at every level, including entry-level professionals, clerks, secretaries, and hourly employees, to innovate.

In 2006, Whirlpool was ranked in the top one hundred innovative companies worldwide by *BusinessWeek* magazine. What is quite amazing about the ranking is that five years earlier, Whirlpool would not have been considered for the index.

Today Whirlpool's leaders are sought-after speakers and are benchmarked by the world's leading companies. Three Harvard Business School cases have been written on Whirlpool's transformation and are taught in leading business schools around the world.

Much can be learned from the Whirlpool story as told in this book. We present a real-life story of a practitioner, her coauthor, and her many accomplices who are struggling every day to embed innovation. As in our previous book on Whirlpool, we present a balanced view of what is working and what is not. We are not interested in writing a "good news" story. Whirlpool's current CEO, Jeff Fettig, is fond of saying that we are perpetually dissatisfied with where we are in innovation. That is because we continue to be on a learning curve, and the more we learn, the more we see what we need to improve or what new areas we need to conquer.

We wrote this book as a team, but we bring our own perspectives. Nancy is the insider, the one originally charged with bringing innovation from everyone and everywhere to Whirlpool in 1999, as we describe in the Introduction. Deb is the outside consultant with more than a decade of experience at Whirlpool. We usually write in the first person plural, as the observations we share come from both of us. Occasionally, Nancy shares her personal experiences as the corporate insider, and uses the first person singular.

The book is structured to help you see the uniqueness of the story. It starts with a real-life example of an innovation team, Centralpark; we look at how their innovation came to market and their reflection on how difficult yet motivational the innovation process was to them. The book then looks at the set of rational drivers that top management must put in place to make innovation from everyone work. Part One is an overview of innovation and a hands-on story of innovation. Part Two comprises the "MBA" portion of the book, the portion that explains the total business framework that is required. Part Three looks at what is unleashed in people when you establish the conditions for innovation from everyone and everywhere. These are the emotional drivers, the people side of the book. The final chapter, the Epilogue, takes an unusual turn. As I wrote the book and talked to the innovators and I-mentors (the highly skilled facilitators of the innovation process), I learned that many of them use their innovation skills in the community to help local agencies. It was the first time I had collected so much information, and I realized that embedded innovation inspires and gives innovators tools to use in their volunteerism. It was also written as a tribute to Dave Whitwam, who started it all and who, now that he is retired, spends his time and energy helping create a new future for our communities. It was fun and rewarding to write. We found ourselves smiling.

Origins

This book had an auspicious beginning. We were in Chicago when we got a voicemail message from our editor at Jossey-Bass, Neal Maillet. We called him back and smiled the entire time he talked to us. He wanted us to write another book on innovation, but for a broader market and with an up-to-date story of where Whirlpool was in its transformation. He was current on all the business press stories about Whirlpool and, like many, was intrigued by the story and how it continued to evolve. He was so gracious in his confidence that we could write a story that was compelling and unique that we continued to smile throughout the weekend.

When we wrote our first book, *Strategic Innovation*, Dave Whitwam was at the helm of Whirlpool. Once we approached him with the idea, he was encouraging and gracious in the time and interest he took in the book. Now Jeff Fettig was at the helm, and we were not sure how he would react. But he immediately said yes and also offered any support we needed. We wrote a proposal and sent it to Neal. His phone call to us altered the course of events for this book. He said, and we paraphrase, "I could publish this book, and it would be good, but there is something you missed that really makes the Whirlpool story instructive and exciting. There is something just under the surface, an excitement in the people of Whirlpool that exists because of the way you went about this. That is the story I want you to write." We were a bit angry. We both had a great deal on our plates, and Neal had seen through us. We had been hoping to write this on autopilot. Neal had done us a great favor. He disrupted our trajectory and made us really look for what was unique and valued by the reader. In essence, he forced us to use our innovation skills and tools and put our money where our mouths were.

Over the next month, I drove everyone around me crazy, the way an innovator does, searching for what made Whirlpool's innovation tick and how to present it. Deb was a valuable and insightful force in the innovation process; her organization savvy and knowledge of Whirlpool was invaluable paired with her distance from the day-to-day. We resubmitted the proposal. I was pacing on a street in Santa Margherita, Italy, when I got the call from Neal. He and Jossey-Bass loved the new approach. I quickly called Deb, and we organized ourselves to start. One of my big learnings in writing the manuscript was that it can be quite daunting when your editor leaves to take on a new role. I was fortunate that Rebecca Browning and Byron Schneider did not miss a beat and kept the torch burning for recording the Whirlpool innovation story.

There are always down periods when you write a book—times when you stare at a blank page or completely mess up a chapter and wonder if you will ever get it right. During those times, we were also collecting information from the innovators of Whirlpool. It was always motivating for me to talk to the innovators and hear them describe their innovation or their learning. These times were what kept us going. It was a unique opportunity to sit in a conference room with a team of innovators and listen to them reflect on how and why they do what they do.

Last, we set up an editorial board inside Whirlpool to help us stay true to the story. There are many points of view to a story and many ways to tell it; I wanted to make sure that the way Deb and I chose to tell it rang true and well represented the people of Whirlpool.

What follows is the result a yearlong effort to capture, organize, make sense of, and explain the Whirlpool innovation story as it exists today. A collateral benefit was that as we wrote, we engaged many Whirlpool people. In the process, we started thinking about new spaces for Whirlpool's innovation effort. It was an incredible learning experience for me personally as well. I also gained help from my classes at the University of Notre Dame and my class at the Graduate School of Business at the University of Chicago. My students shed new light and insights that were helpful in understanding how to think about and tell the story.

We wrote this book for all business leaders who realize that innovation is the lifeblood of today's global economy. Any leader, executive, or business owner (including small business owners) who wants to grow his or her company can learn from the tools, concepts, and methods presented. Team leaders or department heads who want to engage their people to innovate can put many of the practices to work. Academics and business students interested in competitive strategy, innovation, organizational change, and team building will also find much that is new. Our sincere hope is that you will learn as much from reading the book as we did in writing it.

Introduction

"Innovation will come from everywhere and everyone, and when we are successful, every job at Whirlpool will change."

I heard the words coming from Whirlpool Corporation's CEO, Dave Whitwam, and I was baffled. He was looking directly at me. He wanted me to take charge of this massive effort. As a director of strategic initiatives at Whirlpool, I had been leading enterprise efforts, but nothing on this scale.

Dave's bold notion was to include everyone—sixty thousand people—in a new innovation initiative. This meant embedding innovation into every system, process, strategy, meeting, metric, product, service, and person at Whirlpool. We would have to conceptualize the approach to innovation, prove the concept, scale the effort, and produce sustainable breakthrough results, all while building and adjusting the innovation machine to keep it on track.

That was in summer 1999, and as I walked out of Dave's office, I felt as if a ton of bricks had fallen on me. Whirlpool was a ninety-year-old manufacturing company—a maker of reliable top-quality "white goods," household appliances like washing machines and refrigerators. We were a mainstay in an industry not known for change or game-changing innovation. What's more, previous attempts at transforming Whirlpool into an innovative, customer-focused company—once in the early 1990s and again in the mid-1990s—had not been successful.

But the need was clear. The appliance industry of the late 1990s was a study in the classic stalemate. A large percentage of consumers could not tell you the brand of refrigerator in their home; the only time they were in the marketplace was when something broke, which could be ten to fifteen years after they purchased it. There was a saying in the industry that old refrigerators rarely die, they just move to the garage. And when consumers did come back to the marketplace, not much had changed—the products looked and worked the same, a sea of large white boxes without much brand differentiation. To add to the problem, women, who are major decision makers for home appliances, simply didn't find shopping for appliances appealing. As one woman told us, shopping for appliances was like "buying tires." Consequently, many consumers made their purchase decision on the basis of price.

The price of most major home appliances had not changed in two decades, yet quality, energy standards, and features had improved, making margins less and less profitable. It was clear to Whitwam and his team that to break the industry stalemate would require deep customer insights, strong brands, and innovation to create unique experiences at every customer touchpoint—from the purchase experience to usage to brand relationship. To get there, Whirlpool would have to transform itself to a consumer-focused company with innovation as a core competency.

Today, as I write this in late 2007, Whirlpool Corporation is a $20 billion company with seventy-three thousand employees, on track to becoming a global powerhouse where innovative products and services make up 20 percent of revenue in 2007, up from 0 percent in 1999. Whirlpool markets its products and services under the Whirlpool, KitchenAid, Maytag, Jenn-Air, Amana, Brastemp, Consul, Bauknecht, and Gladiator brands. We market in 170 countries and are the leader in an $80 billion global industry.

To put this into perspective, Whirlpool makes fifty million appliances per year, amounting to 1.5 appliances per second. Today almost one in four of these is meeting our stringent definition of innovation. As a result, innovative products are driving additional value in most major product categories, and Whirlpool is on track to reach $3.5 billion in innovation revenue for 2008, with superior margin lift from innovation. Such publications as *BusinessWeek*, *Fast Company*, and *InformationWeek* have taken notice. For example, Foley (2004) states, "One way to think of Whirlpool Corporation would be as an appliance company that's innovative. But a better characterization might be that Whirlpool has become an innovation center that makes appliances."

Further, Whirlpool is beginning to migrate the innovation capability from product design to new organizational areas encompassing services, business models, and execution. Most of Whirlpool's innovation to date has been in changing the perception and value proposition of existing products, but there have also been some game changers. Gladiator GarageWorks is a complete solution for the garage and living space that started in the innovation process and is now a rapidly growing new brand contributing to Whirlpool's profits. ("Gladiator" will be used interchangeably to denote the brand and the business unit.) In Brazil, an innovation called EcoHouse introduced safe, trusted drinking water to homes using a new business model that includes subscription services.

Innovation has also transformed our traditional products, such as washers and dryers. Whirlpool introduced the frontloader washing machine to the masses in the United States in 2000 and continues to offer customer innovations, including compelling design; several adjacencies, such as pedestals (the drawers a front-loader sits on); and a complete line of laundry accessories.

To find the business case for innovation, you need look no further than the story of the Duet front-loader washer and dryer. In 2000, all brands of washers and dryers were white square boxes undifferentiated across brands. When you went to a U.S. store (only after your washer broke), the likelihood that you would also buy a dryer at the same time, known as the match rate, was only 15 percent. (Why bother? Your dryer was fine, and when you took the white-box washer home and placed it next to the white-box dryer, they looked perfect together.) By 2006, our match rate had increased to 96 percent. The styling and energy efficiency of the new front loader were so compelling that there was no way that a customer would not want to match the dryer—both for looks and cost savings. That 1980s square white dryer would take twice as long to dry a load as the new aspen green Duet front-load steam dryer with stainless steel features and high energy efficiency. Completing this case for innovation, the average sales price for a washer and dryer in 2000 was $698, but by 2006, the average sales price was $2,398, moving to $3,000 in 2008. This is just one example of how innovation can add value both for the consumer and for Whirlpool.

Whirlpool in an Unlikely Space

If you look at any of the top companies in the popular innovation lists that business publications generate, you will see a pattern. First, most of the top companies are technology companies. You expect to see Microsoft and Google among the top innovative companies in the world. Second, many are younger companies—less than twenty years old. Finally, there are one-year wonders, companies that are a flash on the innovation front but not long-term contenders. You would be surprised to see a company like Whirlpool on this list.

Whirlpool is such an unlikely source as a thought leader in innovation that some people discount us before we get off the starting block. They immediately compare us to Google or Microsoft or even Procter & Gamble. They ask such questions as how many patents we receive a year, how much we spend on R&D as a percentage of sales, or how many disruptive innovations we have launched in the last year. All fine questions, but not the first questions you should ask Whirlpool. A larger group of people realize that Whirlpool represents a different innovation story. They realize that the relevant questions are *How did you change a ninety-plus-year-old culture? What role did R&D play? How many incremental and game-changing innovations have come out of the approach?* And perhaps most important: *How have you made your innovation sustainable?*

Our transformation started with the reengineering of the company to create a slow but sustainable pattern of innovation that grew over a decade from 0 percent balance-to-sale to 20 percent. Along the way, we created a process for energizing an old-line manufacturing company to achieve levels of engagement and passion that are, to some, unimaginable.

Whirlpool today employs seventy-three thousand employees around the world in 170 countries. Our efficiency and productivity are unparalleled in any industry. We have forty-three high-tech manufacturing facilities and eighteen world-class technology centers with engineers designing in virtual teams from around the world. We produce a number of product lines, including washers, refrigerators, dishwashers, cooking products, and high-end small appliances such as the iconic KitchenAid mixer—and dozens of other new products are on the drawing board. Hundreds of innovators in all levels and types of jobs—sometimes where you might least expect them—are working to innovate across all customer touchpoints: the purchasing experience, service, communication, relationship building, and the product itself. Whirlpool is, in short, a company in an ongoing transformation.

How Embedded Innovation Makes Whirlpool Unique

Whereas other companies approach innovation by trying to foster more creativity, generate ideas, or screen ideas as though these were specific techniques, at Whirlpool we sought to infuse innovation into the very fabric of the organization. *Innovation is not "added on" at Whirlpool, but embedded.* Innovation can often amount to unchecked chaos, but embedded innovation leads to systematic and organized chaos. Embedded innovation is the approach that Whirlpool pioneered to create innovation as a core competency. Embedded innovation creates sustainable and differentiated business results by embedding innovation into the rational framework (down to the day-to-day activities of each person) while creating an environment that sanctions and reclaims our emotional drivers unleashed by innovation. There are many approaches to innovation that companies can choose. What makes embedded innovation unique is that it builds a capability that is sustainable beyond any one person, team, or leader.

As you learn more about embedded innovation, you will see that every aspect of it is directed at developing a sustainable business system that creates a predictable cadence of innovation. Innovations can be incremental or breakthrough, but it is the ongoing ability to innovate and create value that distinguishes embedded innovation from other approaches. But focusing only on the business system that sustains innovation is a mistake. Embedding innovation in processes and procedures—creating the innovation machine—is only half the battle. Innovation is truly embedded only *when it lives in the hearts and minds of people*.

Whirlpool serves as one of the best examples of how to embed innovation as a capability in a large, global company. Although it took the visionary leadership of Dave Whitwam to launch embedded innovation, it has been the continued leadership of Jeff Fettig that has ensured that innovation continues to add value, learning, and results to the organization. From the time Fettig became CEO in 2004, his leadership has been to focus Whirlpool's energy to push innovations to extract their maximum value and migrate the innovation capacity to adjacent, business, and strategic initiatives. Under Fettig's guidance, innovation has become inextricably hardwired into the business.

As embedded innovation evolved at Whirlpool, it came to encompass a rational business-based framework *and* the emotional needs in many of us to innovate and contribute to our workplace. The companies who come to benchmark innovation at Whirlpool ask all sorts of questions, but as we noted, their questions tend to focus on surface details: percentage of R&D sales, incentive plans, and the like. They focus on the innovation machine and neglect the flesh-and-blood people who make the machine run. To understand how innovation works, you need to look at the structures and the processes, *and* at what really makes innovation come to life in the people who actually do the innovating. You must look at the rational processes and procedures of innovation, but also uncover the deeper, less quantifiable emotional drivers that unleash the spirit of innovation in *people*.

The rational drivers include a business framework (resources, processes, systems, incentives, and more) that makes embedded innovation sustainable and often requires the reengineering of legacy management systems. The emotional drivers, in contrast, are not created by a company, but are resident in each of us as latent human factors that attract us to create and innovate. Management's task is to ensure that these emotional drivers are unleashed rather than thwarted. Although many other approaches to innovation use *some* of the rational drivers, it is the combination of the system of rational drivers and the emotional drivers that makes innovation "from everyone and everywhere" an exciting reality at Whirlpool.

This book focuses on how Whirlpool uses both rational and emotional drivers to embed innovation as a core competency, infusing them into every aspect of the company—and into the hearts and minds of our people. In our previous book, *Strategic Innovation* (Snyder and Duarte, 2003), we explained how we began the process of embedding innovation at Whirlpool, along with all the ups and downs we faced on our journey. We also explained how Strategos, the innovation consulting firm founded by Gary Hamel, helped us get started. Since that book was published in 2003, Whirlpool's approach to innovation has continued to evolve, growing stronger and becoming more deeply embedded into every aspect of the organization. This book does not continue the story from the first book; rather we focus on how Whirlpool's innovation machine works today. We focus not on how we got here and all the hard work it took, but on the results of that work: the practices, tools, structures, and concepts we use today to sustain innovation as a core competency. As the leading pioneer in innovation from everyone and everywhere, Whirlpool represents, we believe, the state of the art of embedded innovation.

As noted, Whirlpool's approach to embedded innovation has evolved to focus on two key aspects of innovation: the rational drivers and the emotional drivers. In this book, we focus on all the specific elements of both sets of drivers, and show how to use them most effectively in fostering innovation. The rational framework includes the elements of strategic architecture (vision, goals, principles, approach, definitions); management systems (financial, strategic and operations, performance management, leadership, career, and learning and knowledge); the innovation pipeline; the innovators and I-mentors (highly trained innovation facilitators); and execution (metrics, sustaining mechanisms, and value extraction). The elements are interconnected to such an extent that addressing only one—the innovation pipeline, for example—without regard to the others suboptimizes innovation.

The emotional drivers are the personal drivers in all of us that represent an altogether different proposition. These are currents in the human experience that connect people to the ideals of innovation. Whirlpool was fortunate to tap into these currents with its vision of innovation from everywhere and everyone. Emotional drivers lie just under the surface and, when unleashed, speed up and energize innovation. When fulfilled, emotional drivers are self-reinforcing. They create energy and joy in day-to-day work. The emotional drivers are learning, creating, dreaming, the mythology of heroes, and the spirit of winning.

We did not start out to establish the emotional drivers of innovation that are identified in this book, but we did start with a culture that supported them. Much of our insight into their importance comes in hindsight—after much trial and error and a great deal of reflection. However, we hope that the lessons we learned the hard way will help others move ahead in a way that avoids some of the stumbling blocks we encountered. Too often, companies start an innovation initiative that works against these currents of human spirit through misguided command-and-control innovation operatives. They can marginalize the emotional drivers by making hollow promises of enlightened innovation that do not come about. In the best case, well-meaning innovation hoopla without the corresponding framework that makes innovation work overshadows emotional drivers and becomes gimmicky. In the worst case, emotional drivers are snuffed out by limited innovation programs that bring in consultants or geniuses to do the innovation for you.

Testing Your Resolve

Embedded innovation infuses a company's DNA and culture. Changing the very nature of organizations is, of course, not an overnight feat. It takes years of steady and tenacious effort. It requires paradoxical approaches, such as a top-down direction and systems for bottom-up innovation. Top-down systems are paramount to driving innovation. Embedded innovation requires changing deeply ingrained business systems to create and reengineer systems that allow everyone to innovate. It also requires the top leader's involvement, commitment, and dedication for the long haul.

Many companies fail to reengineer the rational framework because they have a short-term mind-set, or because they try to bolt on a new element without seeing the framework as a total system. Another reason for failure is the sheer size of a decade-long job to embed innovation. This often results in program-of-the-month innovation or a slogan-based approach; innovation is on the letterhead, but no one believes it.

How do you move from very little innovation to innovation embedded as a core capability? This book presents Whirlpool's model of embedded innovation. It describes both the rational business framework the leadership has to put in place and the emotional drivers the people of your company will bring to the effort—if you let them—to help you get from A to B. Such a transformation is not easy; it takes more than a few quarters to implement and will test your resolve. It takes persistence. The lessons from the Whirlpool stories are applicable both to enterprise-wide innovation and to business unit innovation. Many people in the workplace today have a need and a desire to create and to make a difference. Embedded innovation enables them to realize that need and desire. Many books discuss innovation strategies, innovation architecture, or innovation pipelines, but rarely as part of an integrated approach. Our book is unique in that we look at these as parts of a comprehensive business framework, and we focus on the people side of the equation, offering equal time to the emotional drivers that unleash innovation from everyone and everywhere.

Whirlpool still has a long way to go to realize its full vision of innovation. As Jeff Fettig is fond of saying, "We are perpetually dissatisfied [because we know it can be better]." The more we experience innovation and deliver it to the marketplace, the more we learn about our shortcomings and where we need to focus. Whirlpool presents a balanced story of hits and misses in embarking on and charting a course to embed innovation as a core competency. It is a story about how much a company can do and should do to reengineer its management systems, how to develop an innovation pipeline, how to set the conditions for innovation, and how to train and support innovators. These are the rational drivers of innovation. However, it is also a story of trust in the people who work in organizations and the valuing of their innate needs and talents. It is this second aspect, the emotional drivers, that makes embedded innovation unique and compelling.

Unleashing Innovation

Part One

THE ANATOMY OF INNOVATION

1

EMBEDDED INNOVATION IN ACTION

Storytelling is the most powerful way to put ideas
into the world today.
                                    —*Robert McAfee Brown*

As we explained in the Introduction, Whirlpool's model of
embedded innovation accounts for both the rational business
framework that leadership has to put in place, and the emotional
drivers that the people of your company will bring to innovation.
Subsequent chapters will present the rational framework and the
emotional drivers in detail. Before we describe those, however,
we want to show you what embedded innovation looks like in
action, close up. One story that shows both the advancements
we have made and our dissatisfaction with where we are is that of
the Centralpark port connection system. (Centralpark is a trademark for the port connection system on home appliances, which
will hereafter be referred to simply as "Centralpark.")

High fives went up all over Whirlpool's headquarters in
Benton Harbor and at locations worldwide when we learned
in November 2007 that Centralpark had won the Consumer
Electronics Show's coveted Innovations 2008 Design and
Engineering Award in the home appliances category. Centralpark
is a refrigerator with an edge: it is aesthetically pleasing and rea-
sonably priced and includes a customizable interface that allows
customers to add digital modules to the door for information and
entertainment. We first introduced Centralpark with the promise,
"Your Kitchen. Your Entertainment. Your Way," at the Consumer

Electronics Show (CES) in Las Vegas in January 2007—and it had been an immediate smash hit. It was even featured in stories on CNN and HGTV. And now all our hard work had been recognized with this prestigious innovation award. The Innovations 2008 Design and Engineering Award for Centralpark is a tribute to innovation from everyone and everywhere—and to the hard work of hundred and hundreds of people.

When we began our innovation effort, no one predicted this outcome. The CES is the world's largest annual trade show for consumer technology, with more than 140,000 attendees. Many innovative products have debuted at the CES, including the videocassette recorder in 1970, the camcorder in 1981, digital satellite TV in 1994, HDTV in 1998, Microsoft Xbox in 2001, and Blu-ray in 2003. The show is the epicenter of electronics launches in the world.

What makes Centralpark so innovative is its use of customizable modules. With our competitors' products, digital devices were built into the refrigerator at the factory. With Whirlpool's Centralpark, customers are in control and can decide when to upgrade digital modules. In short, Centralpark is not a "me too" product. It offers customers a differentiated customized solution in the space that is the heart of their home, their kitchen. It completely changes the value proposition. What is unique about Centralpark is that it separates the buying decision for the refrigerator from the buying decision for digital modules. Perhaps the best feature is that Centralpark is not a permanent part of the refrigerator. If you decide not to add the module, the refrigerator looks beautiful without it.

How Centralpark Began

In early 2006, a few people in Whirlpool began working on closely related innovative ideas in separate, unconnected corners of the company. Eventually these ideas would come together like pieces of a puzzle in a Whirlpool innovation called Centralpark—and the innovators would grow from a handful to dozens and into the hundreds. As you will see, the story of Centralpark is the story of embedded innovation, from everyone and everywhere. It is not about a few isolated geniuses, but many smart and dedicated people from all corners of the company—including finance, engineering, logistics, manufacturing, procurement, legal, quality, product safety, and more—working together to meet the challenges of innovation. There are four phases to the story: ideation, prototype, launch, and post-launch.

Ideation

Hank Marcy, the head of innovation and technology, led a core group of innovators in phase I, the ideation phase. Hank joined Whirlpool in 2001 from Rockwell Scientific. Hank, along with a handful of other people at Whirlpool, believed that refrigerators could do more than just preserve food. They also knew that some competitors were launching halo products—products that marketers use to create "sizzle" on the shop floor but that lack the "steak" that customers demand for such a large purchase. These included refrigerators with built-in televisions and general Internet interfaces.

Whirlpool's customer research showed that competitors' refrigerators with TVs or digital screens were a great showstopper on the retail floor, but few customers were buying them, for three reasons. (We use "customer" and "consumer" interchangeably to mean the end user.) First, the cost of the added devices is too high. Second, a refrigerator may outlast any permanent digital device fad, and customers worry that the device will become obsolete over the longer life span of the refrigerator. Third, some competitors did not base their device on consumer insights. For example, one competitor placed a TV low in the refrigerator door, forcing customers to crane their neck or bend down to watch TV.

Hank started to gather innovators to work with an idea that the refrigerator would be a center for information and entertainment. They included Paul Hurley, global consumer design senior manager. Paul came to Whirlpool from Johnson Controls, where he had worked on minivan accessory modules. Paul suggested that the refrigerator had to look nice without an accessory, an idea that became instrumental to a Centralpark differentiated offering.

In another corner of Whirlpool, Randy Voss was working on an adjacent idea. Randy is a trained I-mentor—one of many throughout the company who had learned a set of embedded innovation tools, methods, and techniques. (I-mentors are highly trained innovation facilitators; we discuss them throughout the book.) These included methods to generate ideas that could be leveraged into innovations, and to evaluate ideas and experiment with them to ensure that they were turned into innovations that were valued by customers. Randy had a long history of work on digitally connected interfaces for consumer products. He had worked for Panasonic and then for IBM, leaving when it halted its home technology initiative.

Randy joined Whirlpool when we were trying to market Internet-connected appliances. He came to Whirlpool for a chance to innovate. Whirlpool had been working for several years on a number of projects to connect appliances to the Internet. For the purposes of this story, I am grouping all those projects and calling them Project Internet. Project Internet comprised several product development projects in the late 1990s, predating embedded innovation. Project Internet did not materialize and wedged into Whirlpool's collective memory as a failed attempt to innovate.

Randy Voss and Mike Kauffman, who joined Whirlpool in 1989 as a mechanical engineer and progressed to become general manager of refrigeration engineering, knew about Hank's interest in a refrigerator to meet customers' digital information and entertainment needs, so they began talking to Hank about adding external modules to refrigerators. Partnering with others who had a dream of advanced electronic interfaces in appliances, Randy pulled some people together and used the innovation tools (approaches that help teams expand their thinking, create the best innovative products or services, and test and launch them in the market) to create a connected group of ideas related to electronic interfaces, which were collectively referred to as WOW Electronics. This concept would soon become part of the puzzle that made up Centralpark.

In yet another corner of Whirlpool were "shelved" innovations that related to customized appliances. I-mentors from one of the first innovation teams of embedded innovation launched in 2000 had generated one of these "shelved" innovations. These I-mentors had worked on a group of ideas called Customized Home Solutions and conducted successful experiments in a handful of retail stores offering various types of options (such as shelves, configuration, and functionality) to customers, who could customize a refrigerator in the store at the time of purchase. Hank started talking to one of the innovators, Barbara Rand, a skilled I-mentor, to bring some of the learning from Customized Home Solutions to Centralpark. The rumor of a concept called Centralpark started to spread in the informal networks at Whirlpool, and it started to attract other innovators; the puzzle was coming together.

In June 2006, while skateboarding with his children, Hank fell and broke his pelvis. As he recuperated at home, Hank started to write an innovation brief that became one of the catalysts for Centralpark. In July, he presented the innovation brief in the innovation portion of a strategy review meeting, while standing on crutches. Centralpark was starting to take shape.

Hank's innovation brief acted like a magnet to pull these adjacent ideas that were under way into a larger innovation. The innovators started to see their ideas bundled into a bigger innovation. Hank began by assembling the early innovators of Centralpark. Matt Newton joined Whirlpool in 2003 as an

MBA intern from Purdue. Bryan Aown rejoined Whirlpool in 2001 after going to work for Dell; he came back because of his interest in the innovation opportunity at Whirlpool. He helped on the business model for Centralpark. Bryan Aown became a trained I-mentor (his present title is director of customer and profit pool revolution). The rest of the team represented equally diverse backgrounds: Eric Johnson, a senior manager of business strategy; Mike Huie, who joined Whirlpool in 1998 working in procurement, quality, and the brands; Rich McCoy, whose skills and techniques include advanced electronics applications; and Jim Kendall, who joined Whirlpool in 2002 with a strong background in industrial design.

If Hank's innovation brief was the first catalyst, a meeting with Dave Swift, then head of Whirlpool North America, turned out to be the second catalyst. Dave came from Kodak in 2001. He met with the Centralpark team in September 2006, after seeing Hank's innovation pitch. Dave had an interest in launching Centralpark in the North American market as quickly as possible. By the end of the meeting, he gave the Centralpark innovators a "big hairy audacious goal." He wanted three working prototypes designed and built for the January 2007 CES in Las Vegas. The magnitude of his request was at first lost on the team in the excitement of the meeting.

Prototype

When Swift stated the goal, some team members missed the date; they thought he was talking about an event later in the year. When it finally sank in, they walked away wondering if they could do this at all. Three working prototypes in four months? Hank told me that by this point they were battling self-doubt and not sure they could meet Swift's challenge.

First, Project Internet was looming over their heads. Some people in Whirlpool had a bad memory of Project Internet and were comparing it to Centralpark, even though the two projects had different aims. Second, the team "knew" that building one working prototype took at least six months, and they needed three built in three months. To make matters harder, building the prototypes would require intellectual property and safety matters to be resolved before the CES. If that was not enough to shake anyone's confidence, there were two other barriers they were not sure how to attack. First, the economic engine of Centralpark required partnering with exemplary computer and digital electronics companies to create the modules. As of September 2006, they did not have one partner signed up. Finally, presenting at the CES was an unbelievable goal for Whirlpool; the last time we had attended this particular show was in 2000. The show is so popular that presenters need to secure space a year in advance. The Centralpark innovators would be trying to find floor space in October, only four months before the show. However, in typical Whirlpool fashion, they met and made assignments and started to work. When facing great uncertainty, Whirlpool people jump in and start working; it's Whirlpool's version of whistling in the dark. Between hard work and raw passion for their innovation, they knew they would find a way to address the barriers.

Other prototype barriers arose. Legal was not used to securing intellectual property rights in such a short period of time, and the department had a long list of projects on the docket ahead of Centralpark. By the time of the CES, an intellectual property (IP) team consisting of more than ten professionals inside and outside Whirlpool filed twenty-one patents in ten weeks, with the first patent granted in October 2006, an unbelievable feat. They worked over holidays and weekends, often working as a high-performing virtual innovation team, to meet the January 4 deadline to file all patents. Rich McCoy told me that in the IP strategy alone, the innovation tools they used included having the IP subteam hosting an online ideation session for all Whirlpool employees, a war-game event, and an innovation workshop.

Part of the economic engine of Centralpark involved licensing the interface to electronics companies. That was Terry Deegan's role. Terry joined Whirlpool in 1996 from Zenith with a strong background in materials, operations, and strategic supplier management. Some Whirlpool leaders were skeptical about the consortium of partners that we needed to make the economic engine work; after all, there was not a long-standing precedent for securing partners from such diverse industries. Finding the first partner was a tall task. Hank and company started talks with both the giants and the up-and-comers in the computer and electronics industries.

The most likely partner they identified, one of the giants, could not make a final commitment in the time required. They finally decided to go with a smaller but growing partner for the first offering, the digital picture frame. Working through these issues took much of the Centralpark team's time and attention, but they were now on a roll, and nothing was going to stop them. They were deeply committed to their innovation. Their attention turned to building the three prototypes for the CES show. Their passion was contagious.

They called on Doug LeClear to build the prototypes. Doug started with Whirlpool in 1979 and progressed through engineering to become a lead engineer. His job is to convert industrial design renderings into safe, functional models. When I asked him about joining this innovation with the odds stacked against it, he took a very humble view of his role. He too had projects backed up in the shop. He could easily have said it was impossible, or not moved other projects to the side to accommodate unrealistic demands for Centralpark. But Doug is not made like that; he likes a challenge, and he loved the innovation. He told me that the idea of Centralpark excited him because he could see Centralpark in *his* home on *his* refrigerator. He believed in it. He and a colleague went to work and created the unthinkable: three working models for the CES. As he said, "This was not like a model that you can just throw in your suitcase. It was three big refrigerators. We had to build and ship them to Las Vegas on time." So rushed was his timeline that the models went on the truck with the paint still drying. Doug jumped on a plane and flew separately to the show to set up the models. It was going to be tight. When he got to Las Vegas, he found that the show organizers had moved the Whirlpool booth from a hotel for last-minute entrants to the main floor of the show's convention center. Once Doug found his way to the new location, he discovered that the desk assigning entrance passes was closed. It was too late to get a pass to get inside. With little time to spare, Doug waited for the guards to turn their heads, allowing him to steal past the guard at the main entrance of the show to get in to finish his work. He got the models up and running without a minute to spare. The Centralpark innovators told me that one of the highlights of the innovation process was seeing their booth at the show, creating a buzz with their three magnificent prototypes. It was a moment they would never forget.

Matt Newton remembers Las Vegas as a blur of new and exciting experiences, and as a test of nerves. "Up until this point, we were talking with the representatives of enormous electronics companies and not even batting an eye. Then it got ratcheted up and the stakes started to escalate. Dave Swift's secretary started calling us and setting up meetings with the VPs and presidents of these giant companies. The pressure was palatable. We were now feeling the need for a new level of preciseness and absolute certainty required to close the negotiations. These weren't just ordinary meetings we were setting up; these people were running billion-dollar companies! Butterflies to say the least."

Two of the people with whom they met were the developers of a mega California housing development with state-of-the-art electronics and Internet services. One of the important channels that Whirlpool sells to is the home builder channel, which is often led by premium builders like these developers. They could be a potential partner on Centralpark for their upscale, connected new housing development. When Matt met them, he was pretty comfortable answering their questions and showing off Centralpark. Later, when Matt found out who they were (two gazillionnaires) and that they were building an entire city, he said that he never thought he would meet anyone of their stature in his life. Centralpark was providing once-in-a-lifetime experiences to the innovators.

The CES was a huge success. We met with a large trade partner, and it committed to being our exclusive launch partner. This partner was also looking for ways to energize this category, and it immediately understood how this was a more flexible path than what our competitors were doing with their TVs in the door.

Later, Dave Swift said, "I was really proud of what this Centralpark team accomplished, because they realized that innovation does not have to come solely from within and, in fact, in the case of electronics, needs to result from partnerships at several levels (base unit, devices, and retailers) in order to have the speed and breadth necessary to compete and to delight consumers." The CES was a real-enough external milestone that it forced the speed that we needed and the different way of thinking needed to be successful in the electronics world. One of the best outcomes of the show was that Whirlpool earned the opportunity to move beyond our key competitors in home appliances equipped with electronics because Whirlpool is innovating an approach in which partners are invited (in fact, expected), whereas some of our competitors are so vertically integrated that if the innovation is not created and built in their shops, then they won't implement it. Whirlpool has the opportunity to create a much more open and innovative offering.

After the show, the launch phase required ten thousand units to be ready for sale by October 2007 and then scaling that number to hundreds of thousands.

Launch

Enter Lori Cook. All was not dreamy and glamorous when she joined the team. She had heard the "rumors" of Centralpark, and when her supervisor asked her to take the lead on phase III of the project, which involved moving from the three prototypes to getting ten thousand units on retail floors and then scaling up to fifty thousand units by mid-2008, she had doubts. Lori started with Whirlpool in 1982 as a co-op engineer and worked her way up through engineering to project manager, working in the technology center in Evansville, Indiana.

She had her own bad memories of Project Internet. She told me that she could not recall any of the leaders of the Project Internet initiatives ever coming to the refrigeration technology center, where the delivery team worked. It was frustrating and confusing to her and the design teams that a project could get so far in its promise to the market without enlisting the people who would have to design and build it. Project Internet seemed more like an exclusive idea that a few people at headquarters were leading. Her Project Internet experience is what prompted her to do a very unconventional thing. On one of Hank Marcy's extremely hectic visits to the technology center, Lori made sure he met with the design team to talk to them. He patiently listened to their concerns, agreed that this was a tough innovation challenge, told them to "push back" if there was a better way, encouraged them, and built trust. Hank, in this fifteen-minute meeting, convinced them that he was behind them and could be counted on for support. Centralpark was starting out differently than Project Internet. Still, Lori faced many challenges in leading the project. She needed to transform the prototypes into working appliances, not a small task. Among her many challenges was that the design cycle to launch a project like this is typically eighteen months, and Lori had half that time. She decided to jump in with both feet and prove to Hank and the team that working together, they could develop Centralpark. Lori and her team rapidly addressed the obstacles.

Now that Lori was on board, she found herself in the unlikely role of salesperson for the innovation, explaining to skeptics who wanted to paint Centralpark with a Project Internet stigma that this was a completely different concept. The success at the CES was not enough. She remembers having to "sell" Centralpark at almost every turn. It was not easy. The rest of the team became salespeople as well, selling it to others within Whirlpool and explaining how it was *not* Project Internet. Clearly, even at Whirlpool, innovations do not receive a special pass to zip through the system.

Lori and her team were successful. The Centralpark units were launched at Best Buy across the country in October 2007. There was enormous excitement from both customers and store professionals.

Post-Launch

Whirlpool appointed Mark Hamilton in May 2007 to lead the post-launch phase of the project, which included the scale-up of production to hundreds of thousands and the development of the long-range business plan. Mark came to Whirlpool in 1995 with an MBA from the University of North Carolina-Chapel Hill. The current business plan for Centralpark shows a significant revenue stream from introducing new and exciting electronics modules fueled by relationships with at least ten leading partners. It also projects a significant profit pool in four years using a business model that includes consortium membership fees, royalties, and revenues. Centralpark is a compelling value proposition for our customers, partners, and shareholders. The call of innovation brought together a team of dreamers and heroes who did the impossible.

This story stands as a testament to what is possible when you pursue innovation from everyone and everywhere. It shows that innovation is not always or even usually the result of the brilliant idea or the big breakthrough. It shows that all is not rosy for innovators, even at Whirlpool, where we pioneered embedded innovation. It also shows that no matter how well you design your innovation machine, it is the innovators who make the innovations work, often against daunting odds.

What Motivates Innovators?

Perhaps the biggest enigma of embedded innovation for people who are not part of Whirlpool is the nagging question about why our people do it. Do innovators get a percentage of the profits from their innovation? When innovation is embedded, all the management systems that drive it need to be embedded as well. One of those management systems, innovation compensation, is embedded into Whirlpool's total compensation system; it is not a separate program. If you start with the understanding that Whirlpool offers a competitive compensation package to attract the world-class talent we need for innovation, you start with the foundational compensation for innovators. As innovation became part of our company, masses of people started to create innovation objectives in their performance plans. It is likely that the Centralpark team's performance and overall pay was based, in part, on how they performed on this innovation. That is the foundation, the extrinsic rewards. The intrinsic rewards for innovation are a different matter and, innovators tell me, far outweigh any monetary amount Whirlpool could give them.

When I assembled part of the Centralpark team in 2007 to tell me their innovation story, I asked them, "If I had a million dollars to give to the innovators on Centralpark, who should get it, and how should I divide it?" My question elicited a chuckle, the kind you get when the questioner missed something so elementary that you are not sure how to explain it to her. Doug responded first with a great deal of pride about his extraordinary feat to bring Centralpark to the show: "It's my job." He went on to say that from his standpoint, if a person cannot get "charged up about working on something this exciting, then you need a new job." He loves an innovation challenge, and this one was huge. He went on to tell me an interesting side note. When the proto-type was built and he was getting ready for the show, Doug needed digital pictures for the display. He loaded pictures of his kids and grandkids on the Centralpark digital picture frame. Because Centralpark was such a hit at the CES, television channels like HGTV and CNN covered it. Doug's kids and grandkids got to see their picture on TV. That meant more to him than anything. While his appraisal and pay for 2006 and 2007 compensated him for his outstanding contributions, he also created his own reward.

Randy said that he came to Whirlpool to innovate and that "he was getting to do just that." To Randy, the pay is nice, but working on innovations is its own reward. Hank added that he too came to Whirlpool for a chance to innovate and that Centralpark was as exciting and thrilling as anything he has ever worked on. He especially liked that they were working against the odds and won. Matt told me that he enjoyed the entire Centralpark process. It is intrinsically rewarding to him. One team member after another told me that it is not about money; it is about the excitement of innovating and bringing something compelling to the market. In fact, Matt told me that following our discussion he was taking his kids to Best Buy for a "field trip" to show them what he helped build. I could sense his pride in the innovation and imagine the field trip to show it to his children. They all said that "opportunities like this are rare, but you can make it hap-pen." I wonder how they would have responded to the question I didn't ask: "How much would Whirlpool have to pay you *not* to innovate?"

When we began our innovation effort, we could never have accurately predicted this outcome. We knew that there was something compelling and very human about the need to create. What we did not fully comprehend at the outset was how driven all people are to create, innovate, and contribute, not only to business results but to efforts bigger than themselves. It took us quite a while to truly appreciate the power of the emotional drivers of innovation.

The team members' comments are consistent with the results of our interviews with I-mentors and their experience with innovation. I-mentors are innovation "black belts" whom we have trained to facilitate innovation teams. One strong theme we found was that the I-mentors never got involved with Whirlpool's innovation process because of extrinsic rewards, such as money, status, or visibility. They sought to be I-mentors because they had an inherent need to create and wanted to do meaningful work, fulfill customer expectations, and make a contribution to Whirlpool and its success. Many also cited as main drivers the ability to work with other creative people and transfer what they had learned about innovation to community activities outside Whirlpool.

Finally, we asked the Centralpark team who the innovation heroes were on Centralpark. There were so many heroes that helped bring Centralpark to market that they could not count them all. There were lawyers who moved mountains to get the intellectual property rights ready. Engineers who designed the product and the interfaces. Marketers and public relations teams who created a "thunder" on the retail floor for the launch. Model makers. People who worked through the holidays to make a deadline or came in sick to attend meetings. These heroes took their discretionary time and energy and applied it to an innovation they believed in and wanted to have succeed. They were rewarded for their results through the compensation process, but their biggest reward was intrinsic and unique to each person. It is true that not everyone who worked on Centralpark pursued innovation as a high calling, but the ones who did made all the difference. I asked Lori for her list of innovation heroes. The list she sent me included more than forty people from a dozen different functions and departments all over the company. And that was just Lori's list.

Hank, Randy, Matt, and others have similar-size lists of heroes. Who's to say which heroes were crucial to the Centralpark success and which were supplementary? To whom would you pay an "extra" innovation bonus, and how would you determine how much each hero receives? More important, how can you be sure that the extra compensation encourages the behaviors you need and does not destroy all the heroic acts you want in embedded innovation? The biggest incentive for embedded innovation, besides sincere acknowledgment for effort and fair compensation for results, is creating the conditions for each of us to learn, create, and become part of a spirit of winning that fosters innovation heroes, but to do so on our own terms.

Embedded Innovation Made Centralpark Possible

If the Centralpark story does not sound monumental to you, consider the following. Before 1999, when Whirlpool launched innovation, several drivers that made Centralpark successful were not in place. First, there was no systematic transformation to create a culture of innovation. Nor was there an environment that expected and supported innovation. The tipping point that we saw in Centralpark would never have occurred, at least not under the banner of innovation. Some of the puzzle pieces, such as Randy's WOW Electronics, might not have existed at all. We suspect that before embedded innovation, funding for such a project would have been impossible.

Second, there were not deep customer insights in 1999 that every innovator could find and utilize. As in most companies, market research information was generally available for a few people in marketing and was not seen as accessible to people in all parts of the company. Embedded innovation requires that market and customer information be accessible to everyone. Deep customer insights and the requirement to start with the customer's needs are clear outcomes of embedded innovation.

Third, tools and processes for innovation were not common across the enterprise. I heard the Centralpark team talk about orthodoxies, migration paths, customer value proposition, economic engine, and marketplace experiment, to name a few terms, using a common language to describe the innovation process. This common language did not exist before 1999. The team could also draw on previous innovations, such as Customized Home Solutions—again, an outcome of embedded innovation and the work of generations of innovators, such as Barbara Rand, that now exist at Whirlpool. I-mentors did not exist before 1999 to help innovators transform ideas into innovations. Creating rich external partnerships in diverse consumer product industries would have been countercultural and probably would not have happened without the drumbeat of embedded innovation. The strategy to execute rapid and stalwart intellectual property on adjacency modules would not have occurred; the focus would have been only on the refrigerator.

Innovation heroes may not have emerged with such passion and dedication to overcome the odds. Before 1999, it was easier to maintain the status quo. Embedded innovation taps into the inherent needs of people to create and to produce something unique and admired. It also sets up a dichotomy that both attracts people to innovation and also makes it inescapable. Whirlpool trained many people from within to be innovators, but consider the talented people who joined Whirlpool from world-class companies to bring world-class talent to innovation such as Centralpark. Many of these innovators told me that they came to Whirlpool specifically for a chance to innovate. They came to be part of the vision of innovation from everyone and everywhere.

Embedded innovation makes all of this possible. Of course, even after years of work to transform the company, it is not a panacea. There were still many barriers that could have stopped Centralpark, and aspects of embedded innovation failed the team. For example, the team did not tap into the knowledge management system to go online and find other similar innovations, the very reason we created it. They had to rely on their memory of other innovations, but the "who you know" system in a company the size of Whirlpool will not suffice. Seed money for Centralpark was hard to find. The team had to do a massive selling job to get some people within Whirlpool to support it—the waters did not part for them in the name of innovation. Overcoming skeptics is still a skill that innovators need.

The other note of interest to this story is the differing ways that people perceived Project Internet. Many saw it as a failed project that loomed like a dark cloud. Yet others saw it as one of the building blocks needed to get to Centralpark. For embedded innovation to prosper, institutional memory can't demonize innovations or projects that did not succeed in every aspect. These have to be seen as learning and, in that regard, as valuable intellectual assets from which future innovators can draw.

Despite the many obstacles the innovators encountered, there was no stopping them. They had a dream to create a compelling customer offering, and they succeeded with hard work and dedication. That cannot happen when innovation is the domain of the few or when people cannot choose to apply their discretionary time and energy to their passions and dreams. Their spirit and energy, not the innovation machine, buffered Centralpark against failure.

It's hard for us to identify all the people who made Centralpark a success. We are sure that the people we have mentioned are not the only early innovators; we apologize if we have overlooked someone. Identifying the people from the early days of Centralpark represents an interesting insight into embedded innovation, the processes of which are porous and organic, not organized and controlled by a central group. In the best scenarios, the informal network takes over, and colleagues join because they are voting with their feet, not because of a memo from headquarters. Although the early innovators do not see themselves as heroes, they are indeed innovation heroes whom other people at Whirlpool learn about and want to emulate. As the

Centralpark innovation snowballed, the team attracted more and more innovators. Embedded innovation that leads to such opportunities as Centralpark develops into a virtuous innovation cycle: more innovators join the cause and do so on their own terms, in turn creating more innovations that cause others to join.

Could Centralpark Have Happened with Other Innovation Frameworks?

Could the type of innovation effort demonstrated by the Centralpark story happen using other innovation constructs or frameworks? Could an effort led out of a traditional R&D group or using skunk works produce the same synergy, level of commitment, energy, and results? Our answer is, probably not, and here is why.

First, an R&D or skunk works innovation framework could never have drawn ideas and energy from disparate parts of the organization the way Centralpark did. These frameworks partition ideas and innovation only in one part of the organization. Centralpark was a success because it drew from so many people in different parts of the company. The fundamental assumption of embedded innovation is that innovation comes from everyone, everywhere. By nature, restricting innovation activities to one group within the organization or, in the skunk works case, to those from a self-contained unit outside the company, obviates that premise.

Second, the success of Centralpark relied not only on the integration of efforts of people from across the organization but on the ability of Whirlpool's systems and processes to integrate and reinforce those efforts. Without the hard work on creating and embedding systems that tracked innovations, made resources available, and produced long-term migration paths, Centralpark probably would have died under the weight of trying to manage the complexity of bringing such an effort to market. Traditional structures for innovation typically do not make enterprise-wide innovation machines available for everyone. Thus ideas and efforts from across an organization, if they do arise, can be advanced only by an act of senior management, not by the masses. If an organization wants to capture the hearts and minds of everyone capable of innovation, the idea of a lone innovator or an innovation office, either through R&D or skunk works, is flawed.

Embedded innovation establishes the conditions for innovators to use the tools and process to create differentiated customer solutions. Building the machine is critical to your success in innovation. More critical, however, is to unleash the passion and energy of your innovators.

How Embedded Innovation
Has Changed Whirlpool

The story of Centralpark demonstrates what really happens inside Whirlpool's innovation machine. It also shows why Jeff Fettig is perpetually dissatisfied; he knows that the more we deliver and learn about innovation, the more there is to do to make embedded innovation a reality in every part of the enterprise.

Fueled by Whitwam's prophetic vision of innovation from everyone and everywhere, the approach we took was shaped by our culture and the transformation of Whirlpool led by Whitwam in the late 1990s. We also planned and created it as we went along; there was no ten-year master plan of how it would work. We knew what we did not want. Whitwam did not want a skunk works of elite innovators. He knew the inherent dangers of moving innovation out of the core of the business; the movement back into the business was treacherous and often did not work. He knew that organizations often reject an innovation created by other entities. He also knew that our industry was ripe for what he and Jeff Fettig called innovation at the core. We did not have to invent a discontinuous series of innovations to change the dynamics of our industry; rather, innovating around articulated and unarticulated customer needs at the core of our business would have a significant impact on our success. Finally, Whitwam wanted to build a competency, so hiring consultants to create innovations or partnering with companies for innovation was not going to work. Embedded innovation was the best way to introduce innovation to Whirlpool. It was the best innovation method given the state of our industry in 1999 and our long-standing company culture. The results have been astonishing. Now, with perfect 20/20 hindsight, we can say with confidence that there is no other way Whirlpool could have innovated.

The results of Whirlpool's innovation are impressive. First think about the number of innovators involved just in the Centralpark innovation. Now multiply that times hundreds of innovations led by people in multiple countries, across the value chain, and in every function, and you begin to get a sense of how many people at Whirlpool are contributing to innovation.

The tools and process of innovation have changed our company. The language and shared beliefs about embedded innovation created an innovation culture that did not exist in 1999. Introducing I-mentors has opened a unique and valued skill set to hundreds of people at Whirlpool. We have trained over eleven hundred I-mentors. There are also less tangible, but equally critical results to consider. Our confidence in innovation has increased; very few spaces now intimidate our innovators. We are working on second-generation innovations, meaning that we have a history of innovation from which to draw. More important, we have a second generation of innovators. People who are recent hires to Whirlpool think that innovation has always existed. Whirlpool and only a handful of companies around the world are into second-generation innovation and the problem set that comes with it. It is new territory to explore.

In financial terms, the results are equally impressive. We have sold over $8 billion of innovative products since 2002. These are products that meet the high standards that our innovation criteria define. Many of these innovations have created significant margin lift. Innovation is driving toward a 20 percent balance of sale by 2009, with seven consecutive years of innovation pipeline value and in-market improvement. Perhaps most impressive is that we have experienced close to 100 percent compounded annual growth rate of innovation revenue in six years. This means that, on average, we have doubled innovation revenue every year.

But what may be most impressive is our engagement of our people and the acclaim we are beginning to receive through awards and the business press for our success in embedded innovation.

Now that you have seen embedded innovation in action, we are ready to take it apart to see what makes it tick. In the next chapter, we will discuss the rational drivers which ensure that embedded innovation makes business sense and the emotional drivers that fuel it.

2

STRUCTURING AND SUSTAINING INNOVATION

The Rational Framework and Emotional Drivers

> You cannot endow even the best machine with initiative; the jolliest steam-roller will not plant flowers.
>
> —*Walter Lippmann*

We are moving from the age of the machine into a new age of innovation, in which ideas and the people who produce them are at the center of the business model. Although creativity cannot be mechanized, companies need a machine powered by an innovation framework to encourage, nurture, and commercialize ideas into innovations.

Whirlpool has spent almost a decade designing and executing an innovation framework to capture and convert thousands of ideas, from tens of thousands of innovators, into commercial successes. Today, as the story of Centralpark shows, that framework is deeply embedded into our business. What does that mean? We often use the analogy of the software installed on your computer. Without a "deinstall" feature, the software would be nearly impossible to completely remove because the software code has embedded itself into an undetectable number and variety of places within your computer. Embedded innovation is equally pervasive. At Whirlpool, we could not "deinstall" all the components of our innovation framework even if we wanted to.

Important as the rational framework for innovation is, it does not produce innovation in and of itself. New ideas and breakthrough results are created not by frameworks or systems but by living, breathing people who dare to dream, learn, and create—like the people who made Centralpark happen. Embedded innovation creates *sustainable and differentiated business results by embedding innovation into the rational framework (down to the day-to-day activities of each person) while creating an environment that sanctions and reclaims our human need to create.* Embedded innovation broadens the playing field to include not just exclusive specialists but everyone from the front line to the back office, combining both the rational and emotional drivers of innovation.

We like to use an auto-racing analogy to explain the differing roles of the rational framework and the emotional drivers in innovation. Having an excellent, rationally designed Formula 1 racing car offers you the potential of winning—but without the dreams, aspirations, and determination of the driver and crew, that potential will not be realized. And without a machine that is adequate to the task, the dedication and commitment of the people will not produce victory either. Both are required. But too often, the machine, which is shiny and easily seen, gets all the attention, while elusive qualities, such as spirit and teamwork, are overlooked. In this book, we want to change that by focusing on both the machine and the elusive human dimension.

A crucial difference between the rational framework and the emotional drivers is that whereas the framework can be imposed from the top down using mandated procedures and systems, the emotional drivers cannot be imposed; they already reside within people and can only be unleashed.

In this chapter, we will present an overview of how Whirlpool uses the rational framework and emotional drivers today to propel innovation and outstanding business results. Subsequent chapters will explore each component of the rational framework and each emotional driver in depth.

Elements of the Rational Framework

To embed innovation successfully, Whirlpool created a rational framework (Figure 2.1) to drive our innovation process. This framework is dynamic and profit oriented. It includes elements of our strategic architecture; management systems; the idea pipeline or I-pipe; the innovators and I-mentors; and execution and results. This framework is the bedrock of the innovation machine that enables differentiated business results.

Today this framework is paramount to Whirlpool's success in innovation. It helps us avoid common mistakes, such as employing a short-term mind-set or bolt-ons of new elements without a total systems perspective in which all the parts must work together. It allows us to focus on the hard work of embedding the elements of innovation because we know that they are part of a total package, not a program of the month or a slogan-based approach.

The Strategic Architecture

The strategic architecture is the road map of the innovation effort. As its name implies, it stems from the company's strategy. The innovation strategic architecture is a set of connected, high-level action plans that guide innovation. It is this strategic guide for innovation that sets the conditions for decisions about how to compete with innovation. It forces people to address innovation at a strategy level before they run to the sexy

**Figure 2.1 Rational Drivers of Embedded Innovation:
The Business Framework**

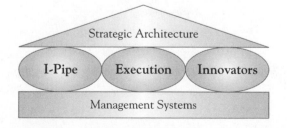

part of innovating. We discuss strategic architecture in detail in Chapter Three. It includes the vision, goals, guiding principles, approach, definition, and process, as shown in Table 2.1.

One of the most critical parts of the strategic architecture is the definition of innovation. It is also the part most frequently overlooked when companies start an innovation process. It is not always obvious why clarifying what you mean by innovation is important. It is not just about words. Jeff Fettig recently told a group of University of Chicago MBA students that before we clarified the meaning of innovation at Whirlpool, "If I walked into a room and asked ten people to define innovation, I would get ten different answers. With that lack of clarity, anything could be considered innovation." We had to have a common understanding of what innovation means and, consequently, what counts as innovation, in order to track increased innovation in the marketplace. Whirlpool uses the following definition of innovation:

Innovation provides unique and compelling solutions valued by our customers and aligned to our brands; creates competitive advantage that is difficult to copy; and creates differentiated shareholder value.

This definition creates the boundaries within which innovation is encouraged, what C. K. Prahalad (2006) calls an

Table 2.1 Strategic Architecture

Vision and strategy	The overarching business direction that compels innovation
Definition	The meaning of innovation
Goals	Measurable results of innovation
Guiding principles	The values that guide the innovation approach
Process	The series of actions and functions that create innovations

innovation sandbox: "free-form exploration and even playful experimentation (the sand, with its flowing, shifting boundaries) within extremely fixed specified constraints (the walls, straight and rigid, that box in the sand)." We will explain our definition more fully in Chapter Three.

In a recent Arthur Andersen survey (2004) of best practices, 62 percent of the firms surveyed said they talk about innovation often or all the time, whereas only 28 percent of the firms surveyed said they have a definition of innovation. Most companies that we talk to do not have a definition of innovation. It seems obvious that defining innovation is critical to the success of innovation initiatives, yet it took Whirlpool three years into the process to agree on our definition.

Once the definition is shaped, it should be operationalized through the processes and tools that drive innovation. For example, one way to operationalize the definition is to use it to develop a screening tool to select innovations to fund.

Management Systems

Management systems are part of the day-to-day infrastructure that drives both behaviors and results. Management systems are complex, interrelated subsystems that include financial reviews, financial reporting, profit planning, resource allocation, operations reports, cash generation, product development, performance appraisal, and knowledge management, to name a few. Many organizations' management systems have been in place for decades and are taken for granted. Although these systems are the backbone of the organization, many companies often overlook them as an embedment mechanism. In cases where companies notice them at all, they can be too calcified or unwieldy to tackle.

Embedding new management systems to support innovation capability is a proposition different from protecting or expanding on existing systems. The new systems must be hardwired into the legacy business framework, requiring both the *design* of the new and the *reengineering* of the existing systems. Start-up companies have only the design challenge; this is one reason they can be innovative from day one. Whirlpool had both the design challenge and the dicey problem of reengineering the legacy business systems that had allowed our company to prosper for decade after decade. Reengineering is the reason that embedding innovation in most companies is a long-term proposition—as it was at Whirlpool.

I-Pipe: The Machine

The innovation "machine" or I-pipe is a set of processes and mechanisms that enable innovators to convert ideas into innovations. This machine carries innovations from idea to commercialization. It often comprises a series of stages over the course of which ideas progress through key decision points known as tollgates. The I-pipe's key job is to prevent too much structure from killing the idea in its formative stages and to reduce risk to the enterprise by building in experimentation and learning as the idea progresses through the pipeline.

In embedded innovation there are two primary sources of ideas, where ideas are just the fuzzy front end of innovations valued by the marketplace. Some ideas originate from a business need and then are adopted by an innovation team. These ideas can come from anywhere, inside or outside the organization. Other ideas arise more organically, coming from innovators who use the innovation tools to produce new ideas. To do this, a team may meet periodically to ideate around a domain, such as water. Innovators then develop the ideas into innovations using the embedded tools and processes.

Innovators and I-Mentors

There are many ways to feed the innovation machine. In embedded innovation, ideas can come from everyone, everywhere.

Innovators are everywhere; you just have to find them. Having a transparent and well-understood process for innovation brings the innovators to you. Innovators are both inside and outside your company. Although some companies start just internally, it is important not to erect artificial barriers to idea generation. To work with external resources requires finding them and on-boarding them to your process in an easy and productive way.

Innovators quickly become innovation *teams*. Today in large complex organizations, it is nearly impossible for one person to generate, scale, and launch an innovation. The greater the diversity of team members, the better the team's chance of success. Diversity dimensions include background, functional area, geographic area, level, gender, thought process, and more.

Execution and Results

Many companies see their innovation process as stopping at the launch phase. At Whirlpool, innovation continues through launch and into the market for as long as the product or service is deemed innovative. Execution involves the strategies for value extraction once the product or service is in the marketplace and the scaling and sustaining mechanisms that keep innovation working year after year.

We focus embedded innovation on results. A virtuous innovation cycle occurs when favorable results beget favorable results. Results become the input for scaling innovation to new levels. The results we measure at Whirlpool fall into Kaplan and Norton's balanced scorecard categories: financial, customer, employee, and the business processes perspectives (Kaplan and Norton, 2005).

The Five Emotional Drivers

Whirlpool was fortunate to tap into the currents of emotional drivers with its vision of innovation from everywhere and everyone. Emotional drivers connect people to innovation ideals and are deeply rooted in the human experience. Emotional drivers create energy and joy from daily work. They are currents lying just under the surface that, when enabled, accelerate and energize innovation. They are the foundation for intrinsic motivation. The emotional drivers of embedded innovation include learning and creating, dreaming, the mythology of heroes, and the spirit of winning. Once you know about the emotional drivers, you can see them come to life as individuals talk about their need to be included in innovation. Following is an excerpt from the *Fast Company* innovation blog (De Cagna, 2005) that represents the need to be included in innovation.

> **If I'm not "personally brilliant," is there a role for me to play in the work of innovation?**
>
> I certainly hope and believe the answer is yes. If we're going to talk about distributed, collaborative "open innovation" that transcends the old-school proprietary R&D approach, then we need to think about how to make innovation as inclusive as possible, allowing everyone to connect to the work in ways that feel personally authentic to those individuals. I don't believe that we should try to limit involvement in innovation (intentionally or otherwise) to only the select few people who possess the "right" combination of genetic traits, personal attributes or learned skills.
>
> As I wrote in a post yesterday, not everyone working on innovation needs to be a wild-eyed, right-brain creative power-brainstomer/prototyper. Innovation demands all kinds of talents, and I think we should look for ways to capitalize on all of them. Our organizations truly cannot afford to waste any brain cells!

When our former CEO, Dave Whitwam, chose the path of innovation from everyone, our effort rode on the wave of the emotional drivers that underscore inclusive innovation. The awakening of our emotional drivers has taken hold through our language, through new practices, and in the way we work together to innovate for our customers. Innovation from everyone and everywhere produced a buzz. Other strategic initiatives, such as cost reduction, reengineering, or lean enterprise, do not share the same set of emotional drivers. The emotional drivers' unique mix of learning, creating, and dreaming, along with heroes and a spirit of winning, are new in the history of transforming industries. Whirlpool's experience has been that they lead to engagement beyond anything we have ever seen.

Learn

We recently asked the innovators and I-mentors at Whirlpool to talk about their personal experiences in innovation. We culled through their feedback with an "emotional driver" lens and found some uplifting and important insights. The most prominent theme we found was on the role of learning and contributing in innovation.

Learning is both an input and output of embedded innovation. One innovator passionately declared, "We all have ideas inside of us. The innovation processes teach us to focus and express those ideas."

Learning to think longer term and beyond the day-to-day pressures was a key story we heard. One innovator said that the innovation tools helped her in her day-to-day work but also on the longer-term aspects of her job. One innovator commented that innovation brought learning and "fresh air" to the business. Many people commented that innovation helped them expand their thinking in ways that nothing else could. One person had a personal development objective to improve his strategic thinking. He said he had not been able to figure out how he was going to work on this developmental objective until he was introduced to innovation. He learned strategic thinking through his innovation projects.

Many respondents said that innovation helped them learn about Whirlpool. One new hire said, "[Innovation] was a great way for me to quickly learn about how Whirlpool works as an organization, including understanding its innovation DNA and processes, but also learning its organization structure." One engineer commented that it helped him understand the whole product development process, not just his part.

Many comments were on the innovation process and the ability to learn how to create different solutions and get out of our traditional thinking. Another innovator liked the learning in a "nonstructured" environment that innovation offers.

The act of learning innovation can transform pedestrian problems into exciting ones. One innovator talked about an innovation session he led on oven racks. By his admission, "oven racks are not all that exciting." Nonetheless, he led an innovation team to look at new functions and design for oven racks. "It's like, how can you innovate around something as mundane as oven racks, but by using the [innovation] tools you can. And the energy in the session was contagious— folks were building on each other's ideas and getting excited." Learning is contagious.

One innovator described the learning and excitement he experienced while working on Centralpark. "As I worked on the team to develop this as an innovation project, I met and interacted with people from all over the company. The common denominator throughout the project was a shared sense of excitement about creating something very new and useful for our customer." Learning is vital to innovators.

Dream

As chairman and CEO for Whirlpool from 1986 to 2004, Dave Whitwam was a visionary leader who often mentored top talent in the company. At the beginning of a mentoring relationship, he asked each mentee the same question: "How often do you look out the window and dream?" The question dumbfounded the mentee; it seemed so out of context.

Whitwam understood two basic things about dreams: dreaming is essential to the success of the enterprise, yet people hardly ever get the chance to dream at work. For the proponents of embedded innovation, innovation provides an outlet for large numbers of people to dream. Dreams create ideas. Ideas become innovations. Dreaming is an emotional driver that attracts us to innovation when innovation is open to anyone. For the skeptics, thinking about a company of dreamers is foolish; as one person benchmarking Whirlpool sarcastically panned, "Do you tell your shareholders that you have a company of starry-eyed dreamers gazing out the windows?"

Dreams can be about innovations, but they can also be about things closer to home. Embedded innovation creates new career paths for innovation professionals the way that Six Sigma does for black belts. One I-mentor told me that his dream was to "get out." When I asked him what he meant by that, he said that he believes innovation offers new career paths that are fun and challenging, and a way out of his frustrated career. He said that being an I-mentor is like joining the military and seeing the world. He gets exposure to so much more of Whirlpool's business by facilitating innovation sessions for different parts of the value chain.

Gladiator GarageWorks is the best example of a new business model that originated from the embedded innovation process as a group dream. Gladiator started by overturning ninety-plus years of orthodoxy at Whirlpool: our targeted customers are women. What if our targeted customers were men? That question has led to a new brand that is the poster child for Whirlpool innovation.

The idea for Gladiator products came from a core group of five or six innovators and quickly spread to an entire department of about twenty. The Gladiator brand started as a garage appliance idea, but it quickly turned into a suite of garage organization and living space products, including storage units, workbenches, refrigerators, trash compactors, and more. Pam Rogers was part of the core team. She reflects, "Some of us got very excited about it. . . . We thought this could be a big deal, so besides working on our regular jobs, which were very demanding, we worked like crazy to make this go." Yet some people in the department did not get as excited. They worked on it, but not in their off hours and not with the joy and excitement the core team did. The freedom to invest your time and the choice to work at varying levels of intensity based on your passion were as new as the innovation itself. Pam added, "When I think about it, it was both a pain in the neck and really, really fun. It was one of the best experiences I have had at Whirlpool, especially seeing it launch and the excitement it is causing in the marketplace. It's great knowing that I was there at the beginning and that it has become such a huge success."

A diverse team of people started the Gladiator brand: men and women of varying backgrounds, functions, and levels. It started as a dream that the team was passionate about, and progressed only because of their energy and by their enlisting more and more innovators to their dream. Gladiator products represent embedded innovation at its best—everyone involved and contributing in an environment that sanctions and reclaims his or her human need to create.

Create

One of the basic underpinnings of looking for innovation from everyone and everywhere is the premise that people are inherently creative and have the desire, skills, and need to create and innovate. At Whirlpool, our job is to create an environment where creativity can be expressed. As noted earlier, the emotional drivers are not imposed, but unleashed.

Alloyd Blackmon's experience is indicative of Whirlpool's approach to innovation. In most companies, Alloyd would not be included in innovation; she was not an external consultant, she did not have a big budget or resources assigned to her, and she was not in marketing or a senior leadership role. Yet she was on the first I-team in North America, coming to the team as the operations manager for our Tulsa, Oklahoma, cooking factory. Alloyd dreamed of a product to help people keep medicine that required refrigeration close to their living spaces, but not in their kitchen refrigerator sharing space with the family's food.

In the early part of the process, she realized that her experience on the team was going to be very different from anything that she had encountered in her twelve years at Whirlpool. She reflects on that experience now with some amazement. "I often think about two things from that time period. There was no turf. We were all thrown into this new area with lots of uncertainty and pressure, but we never once had a turf battle. The second thing I think about is that innovation gave us permission to create. It was OK to goof off a bit and think about new things. Innovation supports our need to create."

Creation as a team starts with a physical space for innovation. The first innovation teams had permanent spaces for their innovation work. These teams set up their own innovation spaces, referred to as discovery centers. The teams were assigned scarce conference rooms or adjoining open office space. Corporate facilities issued them the basic office rations: desks, chairs, and computers. Giuseppe Geneletti was on the first I-team in Europe. He remembers the team setting up its innovation space in Italy (the European regional headquarters) in a creative environment that had many advantages over the work spaces in other Whirlpool facilities.

> In our discovery center, everyone had the same set-up whether you came from a vice president role or a junior role. We all had the same desk, phone, and PC. We had a continuous open office, and we rearranged the space to fit the flow of the innovation process unlike the stable, rigid structure that we had in our

previous jobs. We had an emphasis on technology because we knew we would be doing a lot of research. We had access to the Internet without restriction; unprecedented at the time. Digital cameras became our favorite toy; we took pictures of everything, including the hundreds of sticky notes that we generated in our ideation sessions.

It is interesting to see Giuseppe's emphasis on the creative space versus the noncreative spaces that were found in most locations at Whirlpool and the notion of unadulterated freedom, fun, and spirit of play paired with the removal of standard office management norms. He closed by adding that there was a "strong feeling to be living a very different experience, almost like a hippie community of the 60s . . . but very focused on making innovation fly." I am sure that had the team been issued "official" space in which to innovate, it would not have been as successful.

Today the innovation teams are not co-located in creative shared spaces because innovation is embedded into the business, yet these creative spaces appear as virtual tents of innovation activity almost on demand. They pop up around the innovation work, much like a traveling circus that is built in one venue and then deconstructed, only to reappear at the next. When you go into an innovation session, there are toys around the room, and flip-chart paper is plastered to the walls and covered with hundreds of clustered sticky notes. Team members fill the walls with pictures, migration paths, and elevator speeches. The playground is transient. It springs up everywhere—conference rooms, offices, training rooms, and any other space available. The lesson we continue to learn is that innovators don't need to come to an innovation space—innovation goes to the innovators.

The creative environment of innovation is a messy, chaotic swirl of energy. The innovation spaces advertise fun, play, and something different from traditional work. Whereas many other innovation approaches may offer this playground experience to an exclusive set of innovators, embedded innovation creates the potential for anyone to experience it. It would be another model altogether to have a designed innovation space where people go to innovate. The former is more representative of embedded innovation.

Heroes

Embedded innovation has its own mythology comprising heroes, fame, legend, and storytelling. And as with heroes in ancient mythology, there are highs and lows in their quest. Josh Gitlin was the innovation lead on the high-profile innovation known as Inspired Chef ("Inspired Chef" will hereafter be used interchangeably to denote the brand and the business unit). The idea was first conceived in 2000, and it progressed through our innovation pipeline to market launch in 2001. It was the first large-scale and visible innovation that Whirlpool launched.

Once the Inspired Chef program achieved a modicum of success, Josh and his team were treated as innovation heroes. All the elements of fame encircled the team. They were talked about, written about, visited, photographed, quoted, promoted, and copied. One of their bold internal reports on lessons learned stated, "Don't become distracted by appeasing the corporate gods." Only innovation heroes of the people could speak such corporate blasphemy, only to become even more famous.

Spirit

The final emotional driver is spirit. Whereas the others are inputs, spirit is an output of embedded innovation, and it creates a virtuous cycle. The more that innovation is successful, the greater the number of people who want to be a part of it.

The more people join, the more spirit of winning that innovation creates. Once it starts, it becomes contagious.

Every person wants to win at his or her job and to work for a company that is a winner. Winning creates pride. It is insufficient merely to "not lose." In successful innovation, people approach every task with a competitive spirit. It is no secret that people love to win for themselves but also for a company that engenders a spirit of winning.

The spirit of winning was in evidence in July 2003, as an amiable innovation team from Oxford, Mississippi, drove a brand-new premium SUV to Whirlpool University in Covert, Michigan, with their innovation in the cargo hold. They set up their innovation in the parking lot and waited for the conference inside to end. The CEO, COO, and top fifty executives from around the world were inside attending a strategy conference. The innovation team that came to see them included two engineers and a factory manager from our Oxford factory, which makes cooking products.

Ole Miss had inspired a group of fans at Whirlpool to think about how to solve the nagging problem of better tailgating. The team was working on an innovation called Gatorpak, a portable grill and food preparation unit that slid out of the back of an SUV for tailgate parties and could be customized with the owner's favorite college football team colors, mascot, and fight song, in addition to tailgating options. The team's value proposition promised, "Fun, Organization, Convenience, Save money from eating out, Time savings, and Customized solution for their on-the-go food needs." Then they added, "This is an exciting and fun appliance you will want to show off to your friends! We put the FUN back into FUNctional!"

Being savvy first-time innovators, they changed the Gatorpak school colors from the blue and red of Ole Miss, their local prototype, to the red and white of Wisconsin, Whitwam's alma mater. Once the meeting ended and the participants were milling around waiting for dinner, the team attracted them to the

SUV and showcased their innovation. The Gatorpak innovators discharged their Gatorpak elevator speech with so much pride and conviction that many of the executives wanted to buy one on the spot. Their innovation suddenly introduced the Gatorpak innovation team to leaders from everywhere in the world.

They did not have marketing backgrounds, consulting pedigrees, or Silicon Valley start-up experience. But they did have spirit. Whirlpool gave them only encouragement with an open door, some seed money, and user-friendly innovation tools to create their innovation and test their dream. But the dream came from them. Because of their success, they were talked about in every corner of the Whirlpool globe for their excitement, passion, and dedication to their dream. Sadly, after much trial and error, we shelved the innovation for safety reasons, but the team's experience was unprecedented. One of the lessons of embedded innovation that all innovators must learn is that not all innovations will make it to market, but the lessons learned from each, and the experiences gained, are valuable. If that is understood, innovations that both succeed and fail lead to innovative spirit in the enterprise.

How Emotional Drivers Create a Virtuous Cycle

Emotional drivers are unique factors in embedded innovation. When innovation comes from everywhere and everyone in an inclusive and skill-building way, emotional drivers increase. Learning, creating, and dreaming are inputs to innovation. At first, people hesitate to express their dreams. It takes success to show people that dreaming is encouraged and accepted in the workplace. Learning, heroes, and spirit are outputs that become inputs and step innovation up to the next level of success. Emotional drivers beget a virtuous cycle that propels innovation toward sustainable success.

The emotional drivers of embedded innovation create a unique web that attracts people to it. As we will discuss in more detail later in the book, the multiple intersections of *learn*, *create*, *dream*, *heroes*, and *spirit* come together to create a compelling environment for innovation. Supported by the rational framework, the web becomes a wide net to cast for people who want to be part of innovation.

In a democracy, every adult citizen is entitled to vote (voting from everyone and everywhere), but far less than 100 percent of the people actually vote. The same is true of embedded innovation. We are far from fulfilling our dream of having innovation from everyone and everywhere, but we have built a scalable infrastructure and created an environment that allows for more and more innovation from increasing numbers of innovators. As one of my students said, embedded innovation moves innovation from a privilege to a right.

When companies make everyone eligible for innovation and provide them with equal access to resources, knowledge, and tools, incalculable intrinsic rewards are possible. The intrinsic rewards include the fun and joy of creativity, a chance to be recognized by peers, and the spirit of knowing that you are learning and doing something important and contributing to the company's success in a real and meaningful way. The intrinsic rewards of embedded innovation flow from the human needs, dreams, and desires that attract us to innovation in the first place and can have a place at work when innovation is open to everyone and everywhere.

There Are Two Sides, and Both Are Needed

The best thinking on brand building now espouses an approach that focuses on both the rational and emotional drivers of brand loyalty. If you work only on the rational axis, you will miss some of the key drivers of customers' decisions to purchase and be loyal to your brand. In Whirlpool's research, we have found that the emotional drivers are twice as important for creating customer loyalty as the rational drivers.

As is the case with customer loyalty, many business initiatives require an "and," not "or," approach. They require that leaders use both sides of their brain. There is a popular belief that humans are either left-brain or right-brain dominant. Left-brain dominance stresses analytical and logical thinking; it is the rational side. Right-brain dominance stresses conceptual, intuitive thinking; it is the emotional side. According to Drucker (2002), innovators use both the right and left sides of their brain. The examples of both customer loyalty and innovation require an ambidextrous approach.

The embedded innovation approach also starts with this notion, that there is a rational side and an emotional side. The rational side we refer to as the rational framework. It is the infrastructure required to drive success when embedding innovation into an existing business. The emotional drivers are embedded in each of us as humans; they are latent factors that many companies have stifled through years of productivity gains and zero-variance initiatives. Although these productivity initiatives are critical to an organization's success, they cannot be permitted to eradicate innovation. Successful businesses require both innovation and productivity. A *BusinessWeek* cover article says it all: "At 3M, a Struggle Between Efficiency and Creativity" (Hindo, 2007).

Depending on your preference, you will gravitate to one side or the other. Left-brain-dominant people focus on the rational framework side, the hard business side of innovation. Right-brain-dominant people go immediately to the emotional drivers, the people side of the schema.

Remember, however, that embedded innovation needs a whole-brain approach. Few companies have navigated the strait of embedded innovation by reengineering the framework *and* tapping into the emotional drivers of people in their organizations, as Whirlpool has.

More than anything, embedded innovation is about building an innovation machine powered by the energy and passion of the innovators, thereby creating a virtuous cycle of value creation. It engenders bottom-line results by unleashing and nurturing the hearts and minds of innovators.

Part Two

RATIONAL DRIVERS

3

THE STRATEGIC ARCHITECTURE

I would like my architecture to inspire people to use
their own resources, to move into the future.
—*Tadao Ando*

Steve Jobs of Apple once said of innovation at Apple that
the system is that there is no system ("The Seed of Apple's
Innovation," 2004). However, most mature companies, especially non-high-tech companies, need a system to innovate. The
system for embedded innovation takes the shape of the business framework. Although some companies like to rush ahead
and just start brainstorming and innovating, that approach is
unlikely to yield a long-term, sustainable capacity for innovation, unless it is guided by a coherent strategy and supported by
management systems. So it is important to focus on the strategic
architecture that will guide and support innovation at the outset, even though it will evolve over time.

Developing the strategic architecture for your company starts
with making choices about the vision and strategy, definition,
goals, and principles of embedded innovation. For Whirlpool,
this includes showing how innovation relates to the long-term
company strategy. We do not see innovation as an end it itself,
but as a means to achieving our larger strategic goals. Once the
strategic architecture has been established, it must be imple-
mented through the management systems that drive innovation
behavior and outcomes.

Using the metaphor of a home, the strategic architecture is
the architect's blueprint that considers the homeowner's dreams,

budget, purpose, and uses of his or her home. By contrast, the management systems are the frame, walls, windows, wiring, heating, cooling, and plumbing systems of the house. Much of the strategic architecture and management system is invisible, overlooked until they stop working or fail to keep up with the lifestyle of the homeowner.

Although the top leaders must be accountable for innovation, embedded innovation requires an innovation architect or architects to design and deploy the various parts of embedded innovation. Innovation architects are accountable for recommending an innovation strategy and setting the resources in motion to deploy innovation. Over time, they are the overseers of the tracking and reporting and are responsible for helping the business leaders embed innovation.

Strategic architecture is the long-term plan that includes the integrated components required to achieve the business deliverables. At Whirlpool, our objective is to create customer loyalty to our brands in order to achieve profitable growth. When carefully crafted, the strategic architecture (see Table 3.1) is the blueprint for business performance and results.

Whatever shape the strategic architecture for embedding innovation takes, it must recognize that embedding innovation as a core competency is a long-term process with a significant learning curve. To explain the dynamics of the process to the senior leaders at Whirlpool, we created a chart we call the Embedded Innovation S-Curve (Figure 3.1).

Table 3.1 Strategic Architecture

Vision and strategy	The overarching business direction that compels innovation
Definition	The meaning of innovation
Goals	Measurable results of innovation
Guiding principles	The values that guide the innovation approach
Process	The series of actions and functions that create innovations

Figure 3.1 The Embedded Innovation S-Curve

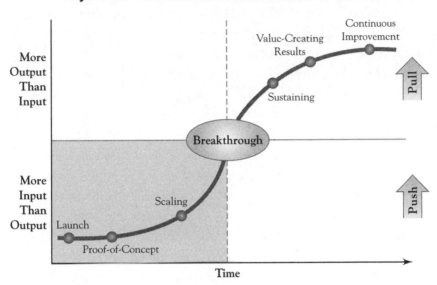

Embedding innovation starts with the launch phase, which includes the plan to create the rational framework, beginning with the strategic architecture. For Whirlpool this phase started in fall 1999; the official launch of the embedment plan was in January 2000. The next phase is proof-of-concept, when the approach is tested. In that same year, we took seventy-five people off their jobs and assigned them to the innovation team to learn the tools and process of innovation. Their role was to learn the tools and become a virus of sorts either by using the tools to create innovations or by helping others learn the tools.

By 2002, we entered the next phase, scaling. This is the phase in which most companies fail. It involves putting scaling mechanisms in place to migrate and generalize innovation to the entire company. In Whirlpool's case, this involved creating I-mentors, I-boards (SBU-level deployment groups charged with encouraging innovation and removing innovation barriers), the I-pipe, and other scaling mechanisms that we will discuss later in the book. From launch to breakthrough (in the shaded portion of the

S-curve), we focused on input measures because that is all we had to gauge our progress. Input measures included how many people we trained, how much investment we made in innovation, how much capital we started to convert to innovation, and how many management systems we were adapting to drive the effort.

By 2005, we had hit the tipping point of breakthrough. We could now start rigorously measuring the results. Innovations were in the market, and we could begin to track revenue from these products and services. The revenues were starting to add up, and we were seeing other tangible results from our effort. It has taken Whirlpool almost a decade to get to the sustaining phase.

Introducing innovation into an older company requires both a push and a pull strategy, with more emphasis on the push. To drive innovation, companies have to *reengineer* their legacy rational frameworks and simultaneously *create* a rational framework to drive innovation. In the shaded quadrant of the S-curve, there is a massive push required to make the changes to allow people to innovate. The push is on the systems, the pull is from the people. Forceful as the push is before breakthrough, the pull exerts equal force on the other side of breakthrough: distributed leadership emerges. People have taken over innovation and are driving it in unimaginable and almost untraceable ways.

Whirlpool created the S-curve for innovation embedment, but as we garnered lessons from the embedding process, our S-curves for other equally large business initiatives (cost and quality, to name two) took less time to execute. If you can learn from the lessons of Whirlpool and other companies, your S-curve could take half the time.

Whatever the length of time you project to reach the breakthrough point on the S-curve, you need to shape the elements of the strategic architecture to take account of the different phases of the S-curve, including the vision and strategy, the definition of innovation, goals, guiding principles, and process.

Vision and Strategy

Overarching innovation strategy guides the process of selecting an innovation approach. Without this top-down strategic context, companies and managers don't have a North Star to guide their actions in planning and executing an innovation endeavor.

Embedded innovation suffers when a disconnected vision guides it; the innovation vision must emanate from the larger enterprise vision. Whirlpool's vision, "Every Home . . . Everywhere with Pride, Passion and Performance," leaves open the possibility of innovating around any aspect of the home, anywhere in the world. In 1999, we crafted the innovation vision that nests under our enterprise vision. With the idea that innovation would come from everywhere and everyone, we stated:

Innovation will come from everywhere, from everyone and in everything that we do. Our heroes will be the people who seize opportunities, not just the people who solve internal problems. We will rid ourselves of processes and practices that hamper risk taking and innovation. We will view falling short of risk taking goals as learning, not failure. All of this will allow us to win consumer loyalty. We will value the diversity of our people and their ideas, as only significant diversity at our company will lead to great innovation.

This innovation vision was grounded in a strong strategy to create customer loyalty. Customer loyalty demands unique and exciting solutions valued by consumers. Innovation was the strategic option chosen by Whirlpool to create those unique and exciting solutions. The vision had a profound influence on what was to come, shaping both the rational framework and the emotional drivers. The vision described the scale and scope of the innovation and guided reengineering to "rid ourselves of processes and practices" that were counter to innovation, and to overturn the cultural orthodoxies relating to failure and lack of diversity.

Definition

To embed innovation, you need to move from textbook definitions to your own definition that you will use to set goals, screen innovations, and monitor results. There are eight simple reasons why you need a working definition of innovation that includes specific criteria. The working definition

1. *Helps screen and classify ideas.* Once you start getting ideas, you need a methodical way to select which ideas you will pursue and which will be shelved.

2. *Maintains integrity and credibility.* When innovation is embedded, it drives many financial and compensation systems. Integrity and indisputable criteria in what you are "claiming" as innovative make innovation measurable and credible.

3. *Provides objectivity and standards for innovation.* Without such standards, you will find that everything will be considered innovation, ultimately losing focus on the type and magnitude of innovation required.

4. *Ensures alignment and consistency across regions, business, and groups.* Common criteria ensure that innovations can migrate across boundaries and allow you to compare apples to apples for tracking progress.

5. *Drives differentiation.* Innovation criteria should encourage innovators to keep comparing their ideas to others in the marketplace. Thus they can focus on what is *not* available (such as a non-served or underserved market) or construct a rationale for why their innovation is superior to what is in the marketplace.

6. *Creates a common language.* Common language is an enabler of culture change and creates energy and excitement around

innovation. It also helps innovators share ideas and work together efficiently.

7. *Establishes what metrics are needed and tracked.* The problems of embedded innovation change over time. Using your definition as a benchmark against which to assess the present state of the initiative allows you to see the initiative's weak areas, and focuses your attention on the biggest problems.

8. *Helps innovators know where to focus to make ideas more innovative.* Innovators at Whirlpool, for example, may have met only two of the three criteria of Whirlpool's definition (described later). They may have an innovation that meets customer needs and creates a competitive advantage, but does not meet the third criterion—the team can't figure out how to make money. This tells the innovators that they need to work on the economic engine of their innovation.

The definition of innovation is our Rosetta Stone. The definition also comprises criteria to screen ideas and to qualify innovations so that we can report the results from the innovation pipeline. The story of how we created the criteria reveals the criticality of creating new systems that grow in importance.

Around 2002, two years into the innovation process, the CEO mandated that a percentage of capital would be set aside for innovation. Most product innovations require capital to develop. Once capital is approved for a product, commensurate funding and resources, such as engineering time, are assigned. Capital starts the blood flow to a new product. Projects had to be innovative to receive capital, funding, and associated engineering resources. If the businesses could not create enough innovations, increasing percentages of capital were withheld through the budgeting cycle.

Because the executive committee (the top ten executives of Whirlpool) could see that the new rules for capital allocation would lead to an "anything goes" atmosphere if there was no common understanding of what qualified as innovation, the group started a deliberation on criteria. After months of debate and discussion, the committee had established the innovation criteria—Whirlpool's definition of innovation. To meet the criteria of innovation at Whirlpool, a product, service, or business must

1. Create a unique and compelling solution valued by our customers (end users) and aligned to our brands
2. Create competitive advantage, be part of a sustainable migration path (successive generations of a product, service, or idea that deploys over many years), or both
3. Create differentiated shareholder value

Thus Whirlpool's working definition of innovation is both a definition and a set of standards for innovation. Jeff Fettig stated that creating the criteria was an early breakthrough in our innovation embedment that "allowed us to harness the energy of the enterprise toward something that created value."

The three statements of the definition represent important tenets of innovation at Whirlpool. To have an idea or project judged as innovation, it must meet all three criteria. Two out of three limits an innovation project's chances of getting support and funding. A person can still pursue it, but it will not count as innovation.

Let's look more closely at the words chosen for these criteria. They shed light on the principles and approach we use to drive embedded innovation.

Unique and Compelling

We chose the word "unique" because it means exclusive and limited; something unique is not like anything else. Some definitions of innovation have the word "new" in them. We discussed "new," but we felt that it meant recent or first, and we wanted our innovation to stand apart from the competitors.

The second word, "compelling," represents the idea that the offering should be irresistible to the customer.

We want Whirlpool people to understand that just because something is new does not qualify it as innovation; it has to be in a class by itself. We also want them to help differentiate offerings from every competitor. Fettig states, "If [a competitor] can do it, then it is not innovation." We worried that "new" would mean merely new to us and not necessarily to our customers. "Compelling" is our version of the "WOW factor." The emotional tie to brands comes from innovations that create a WOW for customers.

Valued by Our Customers

For most of Whirlpool's history, we were a product manufacturer focused on cost, quality, and sales to the trade. Over the last decade, we have been transforming into a consumer-driven solutions company fueled by innovation. When we use the term "customer," we are describing end users, both present and future.

The statement "valued by our customers" sends an important message. Our customers, not our internal beliefs, determine the value of the product or service. The innovator is forced to think about the customer benefit and how much value the product or service provides. We believe that our maintaining a customer focus during the process of identifying, screening, and converting insights into innovations is a competitive advantage.

Aligned to Our Brands

Part of Whirlpool's transformation is to build strong brand equity. In the first seven years, innovation focused our scarce resources on our brands to strengthen our core business. Once we felt that we had achieved critical mass at the core, we moved beyond the core into new spaces.

The brand construct outlines the sandbox for innovation. It draws boundaries and helps innovators decide where to focus their energy. We do run the risk of passing over a great innovation that is outside the sandbox, but we consciously made the trade-off to start at the core of the business. We needed some quick wins. Over time, we have been migrating to include innovation in new markets, business models, and processes.

Competitive Advantage

This is a controversial idea. Many people believe that there is no such thing as competitive advantage or that it is fleeting at best. Yet the concept serves as a mechanism to force innovators to think ahead of the competition.

Whirlpool has taken a stand to ensure that innovators compare their offerings to what is available (or not yet available) to our consumers. When we started innovation, there were many parts of the business that did not have a disciplined approach to tracking competitor moves. Seeking competitive advantage has forced us to be acutely externally focused.

Sustainable Migration Path

A migration path is a specific tool that we adopted from Strategos, our consultant that helped us get started in innovation from everyone. The concept forces innovators to look at a series of progressive ideas and to think about the biggest business the series of innovations can create. The migration path plots these connected ideas on a simple map that helps plan out an innovation cadence.

Our thinking was that a one-hit wonder is not good enough; a successful innovation needs to be linked to a steady stream of innovations that will hit the market over the next several years. Once you have defined this path, you can lead the market. As your competitors are copying and catching up, you are moving on to the next innovation.

Differentiated Shareholder Value

Every innovation has to prove that it will produce higher-than-average margins. As we just stated, it is the migration path that helps create sustainable differentiation. Once innovations are launched, we track them as long as they are growing at a specified rate and are delivering above-average returns in the marketplace. If they are not making this critical bar, we fix them or take them off the innovation list.

Interpretation is key in this portion of the definition. What is the innovation being compared to, and how much more should it make? This element is the hardest for innovators to understand and the hardest to measure and track. A simple way to think about this is that in the end, innovations that are unique and valued by consumers will create profit.

Goals

The strategic issues associated with innovation are partially addressed through a goal alignment process in which every region and business cascades innovation goals from enterprise-wide goals to business-level, department, team, and, finally, individual goals.

Goals of embedded innovation generally fall into one of three groups: input, process, or output:

- Input goals are those that help you get up the S-curve to the point of breakthrough. They include goals for training innovators, setting up funding systems, and determining the amount of capital investment.
- Process goals are related to management of the I-pipe. They include goals for portfolio management, time to market, or the value of the pipeline.
- Output goals include financial, market, and people goals. These would include improvements attributable to

innovation, such as amount of revenue, change in customer loyalty, or change in employee engagement.

A wide variety of goals promote innovation. Again, the goals you select depend on your vision and strategy. If you are embedding innovation, you will set goals for employee engagement. If you want to encourage silos within the organization to innovate together, you may set goals related to the number of cross-functional innovations. If your strategy is to employ partners outside your firm in an open innovation model, you may set a process goal for partnerships. The goals for innovation may vary by the maturity of your initiative. Because innovation initiatives often require longer lead times and can experience lags from concept to market, innovation goals need to incorporate a longer-term perspective than do other types of goals, such as cost-reduction goals. The goals of an enterprise are one of the elements in the business systems that will need to be reengineered to ensure that innovation is visible and carries weight. The goals of innovation before breakthrough rely heavily on input goals. Once embedded innovation has progressed beyond proof-of-concept, you can establish output goals. We discuss goal setting more fully in Chapter Seven.

Whirlpool uses a state-of-the-art goal alignment methodology to ensure that innovation goals set at the top are cascaded from the business to teams to individuals. Through this methodology, the compensation system hooks to goals at each level to reward for embedded innovation.

Guiding Principles

The guiding principles within the rational framework are the set of values that describe the type of behavior, both individual and organizational, that is needed to create innovation. The guiding principles are the moral compass for the innovation effort; they help the innovation architects make choices to ensure that they follow the vision and strategy and meet the established goals. There are a wide range of approaches to innovation. For example, some innovation efforts are team based; others are individual based.

These guiding principles are often rooted in the organization's culture. In Whirlpool's case, embedded innovation requires a team effort that is consistent with Whirlpool's culture. If the innovation principles had called for individual innovators—something antithetical to our values and culture at Whirlpool—our efforts at innovation would probably have floundered.

Dave Whitwam's vision of innovation from everyone and everywhere is both implicit and explicit in guiding innovation. The overarching, explicit guiding principle of Whirlpool's innovation effort is *inclusion*. The vision does not spell out the method for inclusion, but it implicitly states that innovation will not be the purview of a few. We are clear that we are building a sustainable capability. We discovered early in the process that the best innovators are diverse teams of people. Figure 3.2 is the chart from Strategos that outlines the guiding principles we used in late 1999.

The first principle speaks to the fact that the focus on embedment is critical when your objective is to make innovation a core competency of the company. Many people want to go out and innovate and get a project into the market. This is important, of course, but learning how to make the innovation process work effectively and scaling the learning are more important. The second principle states that embedding innovation has to be inclusive. Everyone can be involved, no matter his or her function or level within the company. The third principle addresses the passion of people to vote with their feet. It is pointless to force innovation. We want passionate volunteers, not conscripts. The fourth principle emphasizes the need to make information available to everyone through the use of knowledge management technology.

Figure 3.2 Principles of Innovation (c. 1999)

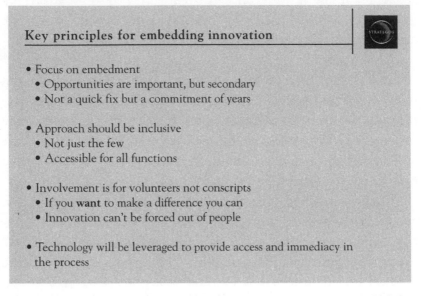

Key principles for embedding innovation

- Focus on embedment
  - Opportunities are important, but secondary
  - Not a quick fix but a commitment of years

- Approach should be inclusive
  - Not just the few
  - Accessible for all functions

- Involvement is for volunteers not conscripts
  - If you **want** to make a difference you can
  - Innovation can't be forced out of people

- Technology will be leveraged to provide access and immediacy in the process

Source: Strategos, Inc. research and field work on Front Line Innovation in Global 1000 organizations.

These principles have withstood the test of time and are still guiding the innovation embedment. Without this moral compass, we would have wasted resources by chasing after ways to attack innovation that did not suit our vision of innovation from everyone and everywhere.

Process

The process is the "how" of the innovation initiative that includes the types, sources, and overall series of actions that create the innovations—the generation, selection, and execution of ideas into innovations. Many companies refer to this as the innovation machine. P&G pioneered the "connect and develop" innovation process. IBM and Cemex pioneered computer-aided idea generation as a key process for their innovation. Some companies use a social network approach to creating collaborative innovation teams. One of my students in the Notre Dame executive MBA program manages a firm that brings networks of professional retirees to companies to provide a diverse set of thought leaders for innovation.

Innovation can be of many types, including new and existing products, services, business model, and markets, as well as process and management innovations. They range from internal innovations, which the customer may not directly experience or be aware of (but may benefit from), to new cost savings, to innovations that meet an unarticulated customer need, such as the iPod. Understanding the type of innovation is critical when learning from another company or thought leader in innovation. When a company claims to be innovative, one must inquire about the type of innovation it is claiming. What is the company counting as innovation—the creation of new markets or the number of internal processes it improved? Few companies have clarified what type(s) of innovation they are pursuing, so their efforts tend to lack focus and to be all over the map.

Some well-known innovators, however, are clear about the type of innovation they seek. IBM pursues new-knowledge innovation. Wal-Mart pioneered innovation in a new sourcing method. Starbucks seeks innovation in services and adjacency businesses. The Apple iPod and the Whirlpool Duet are great examples of new and compelling products. Hammer (2004) has been the thought leader in operational innovation, which he defines as inventing new ways of work. He clearly differentiates this from process improvement or the pursuit of operational excellence through which companies try to remove variance and reduce cost in existing areas of work. "Management innovation" is Hamel's notion of creating long-lasting change in management practices in such areas as leadership and motivation (2007). Whirlpool's innovation focuses on products, services, markets, processes, and management decisions.

Another consideration in the process is where the ideas originate, the sources. There is no better list of sources than the one found in Drucker's seminal article on innovation, "The Discipline of Innovation" (2002). The sources of innovation that Drucker outlines are unexpected opportunities, incongruities, process needs, industry and market changes, demographic changes, changes in perception, and new knowledge.

The Integrator

The strategic architecture should integrate embedded innovation with the larger enterprise strategy. Some companies view innovation as a strategic objective, but most see it as an enabler of a larger outcome. The innovation strategic architecture has to be aligned with the larger strategy and not in conflict with it. The strategic architecture also integrates with the rest of the rational framework.

The strategic architecture is conceptualized during the discovery and planning stage of embedded innovation, usually by the senior team. In most instances, the strategic architecture needs to be carefully thought through by the CEO and the top team before it is made public; otherwise there may be massive confusion. The strategic architecture is scoped first; then you will turn to deploying the management systems, I-pipe, innovators, and execution of innovation embedment.

At Whirlpool, the strategic architecture helped us formulate our innovation plan with a long-term perspective guided by the enterprise strategy. It is tempting to bypass this phase and go directly to creating innovations. If you do, you will probably achieve some results, but more inefficiently and possibly in a more scattershot way than you would otherwise. Your innovation effort may lose credibility if you can't address such questions as "Why are we doing this?" "Why are we not doing it another way?" and "What are we trying to achieve?" Next we will look into the management systems that you will either create or reengineer to drive sustainable innovation.

4

MANAGEMENT SYSTEMS

The fish, no matter how well-sighted, cannot see
the water in which he swims.

—*Attributed to S. Ghosal*

The second part of the rational framework involves management systems—the financial, strategic, operational, human resources, and other business processes that regulate and control the business. For embedded innovation to succeed, these systems need to be designed to function like invisible scaffolding that surrounds the innovation initiative and keeps everything in place and on track.

Management systems that drive the enterprise are usually designed to promote stability and predictability, not the groundbreaking change of innovation. And we rarely view them with a critical eye; they are just there, surrounding us, the water in which the fish swims. To embed a competency, however, you need to become obsessed with getting to the heart of what drives performance and critically examine the pervasive, unquestioned management systems that surround you—*all* of them. Unfortunately, there is no textbook to help do this (and we have not found a class in business schools that teaches management systems), so most innovation experts run to the performance management systems, especially compensation and incentive schemes—ignoring other systems that have the potential to stifle innovation. As we give interviews and public talks on Whirlpool's embedment story, the most frequent question, and usually the first that audiences ask, is about how we compensate innovators. It's a good question, but they rarely ask about the many other management systems that

Figure 4.1 Management Systems

Financial	Strategic and Operations	Performance Management
The thousands of systems that ultimately account for risk and for profit and loss of the firm. *Examples: Sales, forecast, free cash flow*	The systems that create the long-term plan and execute the plan in the short term. *Examples: Five-year product plans, weekly operations review*	The systems that ensure the appropriate set of practices and behaviors that drive business outcomes. *Examples: Performance appraisal, compensation*

Leadership	Career	Learning and Knowledge
The systems that develop leaders through assessment and development. *Examples: 360° feedback, progressive P&L responsibility*	The systems that create career progression and career paths that attract and develop people. *Examples: Technical ladder, job families*	The systems that create, disseminate, and store valued knowledge. *Examples: Computer-aided idea generation, knowledge management system*

promote or stifle innovation. There are many kinds of management systems, and each has many subsets. Figure 4.1 shows the family of management systems that run large organizations. In this chapter, we examine how each can be optimized to help drive innovation by using examples of big and small management systems.

To unravel the mystery of performance drivers, you have to look in some unusual places. There are hidden gems that drive change. For one, look to the question set of the CEO or the top leader. I found that the questions our CEO asked in hallway conversations drove more enabling innovation behaviors than any compensation system ever could.

Strategic and Operations Systems

The strategic systems are the systems that create the long-term plan and systems that execute the plan in the short term. They include planning, alignment, and resource systems that drive innovation over the long term. Let's look an example of a smaller management system, the templates that drive strategy execution.

At a 2003 annual strategy meeting at Whirlpool, the business unit leaders presented their rolling three-year strategies to the executive committee (EC). Presentations at strategy meetings follow a specific format, and if a business leader's plan is structured using this meeting format, it usually has a higher chance of getting management attention during execution phases. In essence, the EC creates a mental action register as an outcome of this meeting. Just the act of projecting plans in PowerPoint starts the process of moving from planning to execution.

I had been worried that the business leaders' plans would not include sufficient innovation execution actions unless the leaders had some help. After much due diligence, we learned that the strategic planning group drove the agenda by sending out PowerPoint templates for the meeting. Therefore, before they sent out the templates, we went to the planning group. After reviewing the templates, we added some pages to the template that required a report on specific innovation areas that needed more attention from the businesses. The planning group sent out the deck with our added templates.

At the meeting, the discussion on innovation was robust. The business leaders agreed on some important innovation steps and spent the next few months making sure that their teams carried out their innovation commitments. In this case, we did with templates what could have taken several months of discussion and alignment meetings to accomplish. It turns out that strategy meeting templates drive behavior. By themselves they don't propel you up the S-curve, but a family of management systems can. Management systems drive behavior, and, as we discovered in this case, sometimes the key to change lies in an unexpected place.

Table 4.1 lists the annual innovation strategic issues from 2000 to 2007. Each year, the EC identifies the top ten issues of the company. (The issues concern more than just innovation.)

Table 4.1 Annual Innovation Strategic Issues, 2000 to 2007

Year	Strategic Issue
2000	*(We used the innovation vision to set and align goals.)*
2001	We believe the customer loyalty and innovation strategies are the correct direction. We do not have the skills, execution, evidence, and sense of urgency that will lead to a differentiated growth.
2002	*(We did not have a separate issue on innovation. It was a subject of a larger problem we were trying to solve related to funding the new strategy.)*
2003	Innovation is required to bring customer loyalty to life. We will use innovation tools to create unique solutions that build customer loyalty for our brands.
2004	Innovation for everyone is required for our strategies to succeed. We are not driving and applying our innovation processes across our total business, nor creating the conditions and processes to embed it across the enterprise. As a result, innovation is not driving or achieving profitable revenue growth and customer loyalty.
2005	Innovation for everyone is required for our strategies to succeed. We are not driving and applying our innovation processes across our total business, nor creating the conditions and processes to embed it across the enterprise. As a result, innovation is not driving or achieving profitable revenue growth and customer loyalty.
2006	We continue to see many signs of success from our innovation efforts. We have made much progress in applying the innovation process across the business and creating conditions, processes, and measures for embedment. However, innovation is not yet driving or achieving sufficient profitable revenue growth and customer loyalty improvement, which requires compelling innovation focus and execution.
2007	We must instill rigor into our innovation process by building a management system on par with our other operating management systems. In addition, we must expand the impact of core business innovation while taking innovation to the next level with new and expanded profit pools.

Articulating the strategic issues is part of the strategic and operations systems. Once the EC identifies the issues, we define them as problem statements and use them to set goals for the next three years. Since 2004, we have put special emphasis on the issues through a goal alignment system that cascades down through the businesses. The goal alignment system is a key embedment mechanism for innovation.

Also since 2004, Jeff Fettig has met quarterly with the innovation architects (the EC sponsor, the global innovation head, and me) to review the global innovation goals and actions. The global head, in turn, meets once a month with a global innovation council made up from members of each region to work on both strategic and tactical issues. This review process is also a key embedment mechanism for innovation.

Goals come to life in quarterly operations reviews and other periodic operations meetings. The business leaders review the goals; the central innovation group tracks and reports the progress. Another part of the strategic system of innovation is the balanced scorecard. Since 2002, innovation has been a key item on the balanced scorecard. A balanced scorecard is a strategic planning tool that tracks financial and nonfinancial measures of an enterprise. When we measured the input of innovation (the bottom left quadrant of the S-curve), innovation goals were mainly learning goals. Once we started measuring the output of innovation, the goals became focused on shareholder value. By 2004, we started measuring the health of the pipeline, and, by 2007, we added balance of sale for the purpose of driving continued innovation efforts in each product category.

Financial Systems

The earlier example of the strategy meeting illustrates the relatively simple action of inserting a template into an existing strategy process. Much of the work on management systems involves investing a more significant amount of time and resources on reengineering those systems to drive innovation without disrupting the operations of the business.

Financial systems are the web of accounting and financial subsystems that account for the profit and loss of the firm. If you have gone through the Sarbanes-Oxley compliance process in the last five years, you are well aware of these systems. Sarbanes-Oxley made them visible as companies ensured that they were in compliance with the new federal guidelines.

Looking at the financial systems of the product development and launch system gives an idea of the kind of work required to reengineer one of the key management systems. For a manufacturer and seller of major appliances, the product development system is the backbone of the business. Using this major operating management system and its corresponding financial systems that track, monitor, and report, let's look at how to embed innovation into one aspect of the company's financials.

One of the most provocative concepts that Gary Hamel and Strategos introduced to Whirlpool was the notion of resource creation. If you think about resources for embedded innovation on the Embedded Innovation S-Curve, in the beginning you will need to allocate resources. Resources include people, funds, and capital. As you progress up the S-curve, embedded innovation begins to create resources, both in terms of revenue that can be reinvested into innovation and in terms of people who are attracted to the success of innovation. Once you hit breakthrough, resources convert from allocated to created.

Figure 5.2 shows the product development system integrated with the innovation process, and Chapter Five will do a deep dive into the I-pipe portion of product development. For this discussion, let's isolate the financial systems that track, monitor, and report on innovative products as we design, build, and sell them.

Pre-Launch

We embedded the I-pipe into the traditional product development process to track products from idea to post-launch.

Although both products and services go through the process, for this example we will look only at products. The product starts as an idea and then is screened to see if it is innovative. The product goes through the product development process flagged as an innovation product because it has met the strict definition of innovation. If products do not meet the definition, we challenge the innovation team to go back and redesign the product using innovation tools. The tollgates keep weeding out or scaling up innovations as they progress through the process.

The financials in pre-launch assess and report at both a micro and macro level. At the micro level, we measure duration of the individual products in each stage, their speed through the pipeline, and projected financials of the product as it progresses. At a macro level, we measure projected value of the pipeline, the portfolio of projects, number and value of projects by stage in the pipeline, overall speed through the process, and shelved projects that do not make it. For portfolio assessment we look at four types of innovation: new business (example: Gladiator GarageWorks), new product (example: pedestals for front-loading washers and dryers), merchandisable (example: refrigerator doors that dispense filtered water), and platform replacement (example: new dryer platform).

Post-Launch

When Jeff Fettig became chairman in 2004, his innovation focus was to hardwire the innovation financials to the company's financials. Up to this point, innovation financials were tracked and reported separately and manually. Fettig's mandate to hardwire innovation had a direct impact on the post-launch phase. He wanted to track each innovation in the marketplace to see if it was achieving above-average margins, per the definition for innovation. If an innovation is not garnering a higher margin, it requires an innovation refresh, or it is "defrocked" and no longer counts as innovation. To follow Fettig's mandate, we had to go back into our automated financial system to manually flag individual products as innovative. It was a painstaking process carried out in each region, requiring many months. Once we had established the platform for flagging product SKUs, the flagging of new innovation SKUs became a maintenance issue and took only incremental effort.

Once we flag the product as innovative, we are better able to track and report results. We can slice and dice the financials to look at different facets of innovation profitability by product, accountable leader, product category (washer, refrigerator, and so on), and region, to name a few.

In one of our quarterly EC meetings on innovation, we debated how long to track post-launch innovations. There was a motion to track them for a maximum of three years. The debate turned us back to our innovation definition once again. We determined that as long as the product "acted" innovative, we would count it. The business manager of the product is accountable for continuing to evaluate the innovation product in the market against the definition, and as long as it meets the three criteria, we track it as innovation. When it is no longer innovative, the business manager makes sure that he or she has the next product launching from the pipeline so as to ensure reaching the business unit's innovation goals.

The hardwiring of the financials for the I-pipe is just one example of reengineering a management system. We could have saved untold aggravation and money if we had known enough to reengineer these systems at the beginning, but it was impossible to know everything in year one.

Performance Management Systems

Performance management systems are the systems that ensure the appropriate set of practices and behaviors from the people of the company to drive business outcomes. The biggest enigma in Whirlpool's innovation embedment story is the pay system for innovation. In a company the size of Whirlpool, innovation requires teams of innovators, not individual geniuses. If we use Gladiator GarageWorks as an example, it took a small team to create the idea, a business group to scale up the idea, and a new-brand group to launch and continually renew the innovations for the new brand. To pay a cash incentive to one or two innovators in this process would be divisive. Imagine being a part-time member of the team and for some reason receiving a partial incentive or not getting compensated at all. It is also important to consider how a company changes as it embeds innovation or any key capability. At the beginning of the process, innovation is an extra element, and it may need to be separated out as a specific aspect of performance that is rewarded for itself. Once the company embeds innovation into day-to-day practices, however, it becomes part of the total compensation system.

For example, the quality movement began in earnest in most U.S. companies in the early 1980s. To embed quality into an enterprise, companies had to progress through the S-curve. At the point of scale-up, companies expected more and more people to have quality efforts embedded in their job. Over time, quality became everyone's job, and companies no longer paid separately for work on quality. The same is true for innovation. At first there may be reason to reward teams or individuals outside the normal compensation system, but the goal over the longer term is to pay within the normal compensation system. Today Whirlpool compensates innovators in a continuous and mainstream way.

It is also important to remember that a too-narrow focus on how we compensate innovators assumes that innovators need to be motivated by significant extrinsic rewards. Embedded innovation creates not only sustainable and differentiated business results but also an environment that endorses and reclaims our human need to create. It is this environment that creates intrinsic rewards for innovators.

That being said, Whirlpool does have a compensation system that can be reengineered to fit the innovation outcomes.

The compensation system at Whirlpool has both an individual and organization portion. It also has a special feature for senior leaders who have the added accountability to build and sustain the innovation machine by removing the barriers to innovation.

Each year-end bonus has two parts, a company multiplier and an individual multiplier. We will look at this isolating the innovation-relevant components of the compensation system.

Company multiplier. The company multiplier targets the company's total result in innovation. The company's balanced scorecard attainment triggers a judgment by the board of directors about how much the company multiplier will be for year-end bonuses. As a result, each person's bonus has a portion of the payout based directly on the company's goal attainment for innovation.

Individual multipliers. We base the individual multiplier on individual performance. We customize this area by how much involvement an individual has in innovation. Although we have not met our goal of innovation from everyone, the compensation system will reward individuals who practice it. Here are some of the variations you can see in the individual compensation.

- The area of the company that develops products has innovation departmental goals and individual goals. A person's attainment of her individual innovation goals enters into the calculation of her year-end bonus.

- If an individual is developing himself in innovation or if he is innovating "outside his normal job," it is likely that he and his boss will recognize these efforts on his individual appraisal. Consequently, the individual's year-end performance assessment will reward him for his innovation involvement.

- An I-mentor who performs well usually has her I-mentor work documented on her appraisal as a portion of her deliverables, which the individual and her supervisor evaluate for pay.

- Teams of innovators may receive an instant special cash award if their work is deemed extraordinary by their leader. They will get an individual incentive in their year-end bonus.

Senior leader long-term incentive. Embedded innovation is both top down and bottom up. There is top-down creation and reengineering of the rational framework so that ideas can come from the bottom up. Only the leaders at the top who control the big management systems can make the significant changes required to drive innovation. In other words, senior leaders have an added accountability in embedded innovation that "everyone" does not.

The top two hundred leaders at Whirlpool receive a portion of their compensation as a long-term bonus. We base the long-term bonus on three areas: economic value add, customer loyalty, and innovation. For innovation to pay in this system, the company has to meet its overall innovation goals over a three-year rolling period. The goal in 2007 targets revenue and health of the I-pipe.

Recognition. An equally important part of the compensation system is the recognition that innovators receive. One important way to recognize innovators is to provide them opportunities to present their innovation to others outside their group or to a senior leader whom they have never met. And great peer recognition can provide a psychic boost for innovators when innovation is valued in a company.

Extrinsic rewards are necessary but not sufficient in the infinite world of innovation. Embedded innovation can offer intrinsic rewards to innovators by moving in harmony with emotional drivers, as we saw in Chapter One in the Centralpark example. The unique combination of innovation and inclusion makes the intrinsic rewards hard to copy. Intrinsic rewards of a cost containment initiative, for example, could not be as fertile and exciting to so many people as those of inclusive innovation.

Innovation allows people an opportunity to engage in their interests, improve their capabilities, expand to new avenues of advancement, and master challenges, all of which psychologists know are more motivating than money alone. Innovation also is an outlet for dreams. Innovation can offer this to the few, but imagine the possibilities when these intrinsic rewards are available to everyone.

Leadership Development Systems

Leadership systems ensure that leaders are assessed and developed in line with the strategic intent of the company. Leadership is critical to embedded innovation. We started to see a new avenue by which to embed innovation: teaching it in leadership development.

The next phase of innovation embedment for Whirlpool migrates the innovation tools beyond products and services. In 2006, we designed and piloted a unique leadership development program titled Leading the Whirlpool Enterprise (LWE). The objective of LWE is to develop leadership and business around real opportunities. We also use a combination of innovation and Six Sigma tools applied in new ways to business planning and execution.

To establish topics for the program, we ask the EC to identify Whirlpool's most pressing problems or biggest opportunities. The following list summarizes the topics chosen in 2007, which ranged from new strategies to next-phase development of existing strategies. (The term *blue ocean* in two of the list items refers to creating uncontested or unexploited markets, where there is little or no competition [Kim and Mauborgne, 2005].) We select the group of people accountable for each topic and invite them to the program as a team. The teams have members from multiple levels and from across the value chain. Sometimes they have never met the other members. We also invite diverse thought leaders to join the teams.

Topics for the Leading the Whirlpool Enterprise Program, 2007

- Fabric care blue ocean
- First launch value creation
- Post-launch value creation
- Regional competitive gaming
- Attracting and developing top talent
- China strategy 2008–2012
- Home improvement sector blue ocean
- Consumables growth
- Supplier relationships
- Cash generation
- Integration of new businesses
- Material cost productivity
- Freight and warehousing
- Total lean enterprise

On day one of the program, I-mentors work with the team to expand their thinking using the Whirlpool strategy, blue ocean concepts, and other expansive innovation tools.

In the afternoon of day one and through day two, the teams work with a group of I-mentors and Six Sigma black belts to expand the opportunity, create new choices, and think about the problem in a different way. By the end of day three, the team has created a migration path of their expanded ideas, an opportunity brief, and a hundred-day execution plan using innovation tools and processes that include an elevator speech. Jeff Fettig and other EC members meet with the team on day four of the program to hear their plans. The participants make a personal and team commitment to deliver a level of outcomes that were not imagined before LWE. The innovation tools motivate teams to move to a blue ocean, reenergize the core business, and look at productivity in new ways.

The results of LWE are compelling and include the personal growth of the I-mentors that become part of the faculty. One of the first LWE sessions we conducted was for fifty-five leaders of the North American laundry team, a $5 billion business. I invited Floria Washington to be part of the faculty for this laundry LWE at Whirlpool University in Covert, Michigan. She works in the Marion, Ohio, division, Whirlpool's largest laundry factory (making over twenty-four thousand washers a day!), so her experience in the laundry business coupled with her I-mentor training were a natural fit.

She later recalled that she had no idea how we would apply the innovation process to such a big management topic. She told us, "I took a big gulp and thought about learning a new space. I wanted to understand how this could work." One week before LWE, she and fifteen of her colleagues attended a three-day refresher session on the innovation tools and a workshop on how to apply the tools to strategy and management decisions.

Washington said that on her three-hour drive back to Marion after the refresher session, she started thinking about ways to use the tools for new problems and started writing suggested innovation approaches that the laundry team could use to enlarge their opportunity. The following week, she and a team of I-mentors and Six Sigma black belts facilitated the laundry business in thinking about a new strategy and creating a plan for platform cost reduction and cadenced innovation. She and her colleagues presented a hundred-day plan to Jeff Fettig and three other EC members from the North American region. Once LWE ended, Washington and her factory manager devised a plan to align her factory's product strategy and goals to the hundred-day execution plan that the team established to implement their ideas. She now plans to lead similar sessions in the factory to embed the process and to apply the innovation tools to management innovation. She said that LWE was the first time she saw such connectivity across the value chain and saw the innovation process applied to a new problem set.

In LWE, the innovation tools were instrumental in creating a differentiated strategy; they also brought people from all parts of the business together in a fun and meaningful way to look for new solutions. When I asked Washington what results she has seen, she said that the actions taken by the team as a result of LWE are now part of the goal-setting, learning system of her factory. Deploying the improvements from LWE is now part of her job. She said her goal over the next year was to use the innovation and Six Sigma tools to help people look for new solutions in nonproduct areas.

Career Management Systems

Career management systems create career progression and career paths that attract and develop people. The talent pool system also has to adapt to accept innovation as a key success factor in career progression. Whirlpool does not use innovation characteristics alone to evaluate talent. We have company values and a leadership model that spell out characteristics of success. For example, in the leadership model, "thought leadership" and "leader of change" are key parts of the success profile for innovators. The talent pool system also addresses attracting new talent. Our belief is that if a person has the great business skills and high ethics that we seek in every candidate, he or she can learn the innovation process and tools. Therefore, we do not screen new hires using specific creativity criteria.

A collateral benefit of embedded innovation is that highly talented people want to work for a company where they have a chance to innovate. I have met hundreds of new Whirlpool people who have highly competitive skills who came to Whirlpool for this reason. One new hire recently told me that five years ago he would not have considered Whirlpool, but then he read how our innovation process works. He came to Whirlpool because he wanted to work for a global company where he has a chance to innovate.

Career Opportunities for I-Mentors

Delivering a program such as LWE requires long hours both to teach and to redesign the next day's program as each day unfolds. I, along with my colleague Kim Thompson, would spend many evening hours with my design team and the I-mentors and then go home exhausted. I would come in the next day to discover that the I-mentors had stayed long after I left, working on refining the next day's events. From the first day, the I-mentors had no expectation of extra pay; they were working for the challenge and opportunities to be involved with something so important to Whirlpool. On the last day of the program, the business teams of fifty thanked the I-mentors with deafening applause for their work in helping them create breakthrough ideas. It was wonderful public recognition. We also gave the I-mentors an on-the-spot bonus for their work, and we informed their bosses of their outstanding contribution and asked them to include the I-mentors' LWE performance in their appraisal.

Something unplanned happened in the LWE program. LWE showcased I-mentors to senior leaders who did not know them. On many occasions, I-mentors received new job opportunities because of their excellent work in LWE. LWE is another example of embedded innovation. Business teams use innovation in new and unique ways. I-mentors accept new, unexpected jobs because of their dedication to and mastery of the innovation process.

I recently presented at a large global conference on innovation. Afterward, as I was meeting some attendees, a man from a Whirlpool global competitor introduced himself with a good-natured greeting: "Hello, I have one of your I-mentors!" We went on to talk about a person he had recruited. I was both sad and happy. I was sad that we had lost an I-mentor, but happy that other companies value them. I-mentors are to innovation what black belts are to Six Sigma. Increasing numbers of companies that embed innovation will value the skill set of I-mentors.

Change Every Job

One aspect of the career systems is to embed innovation into job grouping. We cannot expect everyone to innovate the same way, but we can expect innovation to be in every job. Remember that in 1999 when Dave Whitwam appointed me as the VP of innovation, he said, "We will know we are successful when every job at Whirlpool changes." In 1999, we had no clear sense of how to accomplish that. Only in the last two years, as we have begun to work on job families, have we been able to describe general innovation expectations for groups of jobs.

When we created the role of I-mentors, we set up a new career track. People can qualify for the full-time I-mentor job and pursue a successful career in innovation. They can become part-time I-mentors. Everyone can embed innovation into his or her job. Further, as we noted earlier, highly talented I-mentors are frequently offered new career opportunities.

Learning and Knowledge Systems

The final group of management systems is the learning and knowledge systems. Leadership development and learning and knowledge systems have the greatest potential to create competitive advantage that is unique and differentiated. Learning and knowledge systems create, disseminate, and store valued knowledge. Innovation from everyone and everywhere requires that knowledge be democratized and available to everyone. It also requires a continuous improvement process that enables continued learning and adaptation. It is especially important to collect patterns of learnings from the innovation processes and to share them in a forum. For example, we have a knowledge management system that collects and disseminates learnings that everyone at Whirlpool can access. We also have the global innovation council, which ensures that we share learning across regions. Finally, we learn many lessons from external sources—whether by benchmarking great innovative companies or through our use of open innovation models that include suppliers, universities, and trade partners, to name a few.

Tailor Systems to Specific Needs

Not every company has the leadership and resources to reengineer the management systems the way that Whirlpool has, but each company can size the approach to fit its own needs. The hard work of reengineering management systems is what drives a company up the S-curve, and why it takes so long to embed innovation. But reengineering management systems is also what makes innovation sustainable.

We continually find well-intentioned companies, often guided by consultants, to be heavily invested in only one or two aspects of management systems reengineering but failing to see the entire landscape. Beware the "charlatan" consultants bearing flashy PowerPoint slides. Everyone is on the innovation bandwagon now, and many consultants have repackaged their last paying gig and renamed it innovation. These are the consultants who push a one-note answer: hire the smartest innovative people or build an innovation pipeline or form a joint venture. Very few consultants advise sustainable systems changes because doing so is not in their best interest. How can you make sure that your consultant is going to have a management system perspective?

When anyone comes to pitch anything to Jeff Fettig, he has one killer question he asks to test the person's resolve: "How do you know that this is going to work?" Similarly, to make sure you are getting a seasoned innovation approach, you need a set of killer questions to weed out the charlatan consultants. Here are three to consider. First, ask the consultants if they have ever embedded innovation and made it work in a company such as yours. If they say yes, ask to see the company's results. Second, ask how they define innovation and how they would operationalize the definition. Last, ask what they would recommend with regard to management systems and see what they say.

Systems Are Essential

Getting people motivated to innovate without also reengineering the management systems that drive the innovation machine is tantamount to setting them up for failure. There is nothing more caustic than getting everyone ready to innovate but then failing to change the systems that enable innovations to succeed.

Bill Cosby, the great American comedian, used to do a routine about a high school football team whose coach was charging them up in the locker room before their defining final game. As the coach's pronouncements that they were the best and were going to win escalated to a high-pitched fury, the team became more and more psyched. They were cheering, hitting lockers, and working themselves into a kill-the-other-team frenzy. They were at the peak of excitement when the coach masterfully unleashed them to take to the field. In hyped-up team mania, they charged toward the field in one huge mass of testosterone, only to find the locker room door locked.

This comedy routine is the subtext that goes through our heads when executives from other companies tell us about their innovation bells and whistles but do not appear to be dedicated to changing their management systems to drive innovation. As they talk, we can't help think about their sending their motivated innovators out, only to have them run into the locked door that squanders human and business potential.

We have provided only a bird's-eye view of the management systems at Whirlpool, highlighting the key aspects that support innovation. We do not have the space in this book to examine each and every system in detail—and our point is not that you should adopt our systems for your company in any case. Rather, our point is that you need to take a systematic look at all the management systems in your company—from high-level strategy processes to the nuts and bolts of career tracks—to ensure that none of them create a locked door for innovation.

Are all the doors to successful innovation open at your company?

5

THE INNOVATION MACHINE

Look at the product pipeline, look at the fantastic
financial results we've had for the last five years.
You only get that kind of performance on the
innovation side, on the financial side, if you're
really listening and reacting to the best ideas of the
people we have.

— *Steve Ballmer, CEO of Microsoft Corporation*

Many companies that innovate struggle to build an innovation
pipeline (I-pipe) that creates a cadence of innovation. In their
Harvard Business Review article "The Innovation Value Chain,"
Hansen and Birkinshaw (2007) discuss the I-pipe and caution
companies against making one piece of the innovation value
chain the focus of innovation efforts without thinking of the
I-pipe as an end-to-end process. We have used this approach at
Whirlpool—an approach even more critical when embedding
innovation as a core competency.

The strategic architecture and the management systems create
the conditions for innovation to thrive, but neither creates innovation. The critical path to innovate in the marketplace is the I-pipe.
The I-pipe is the machine that produces marketable innovations.

Innovative Companies Versus
Companies That Innovate

In the first year of Whirlpool's innovation, we chartered three
teams of twenty-five people located in three regional headquarters: Comerio, Italy; São Paulo, Brazil; and Benton Harbor,

Michigan. We trained the seventy-five innovators for one year and simultaneously built the I-pipe.

What is still impressive is that in 2000 when we chartered the teams, Whitwam did not concern himself with innovations coming out of the pipeline. He focused on building a machine for a continuous flow of innovation for years to come. In the early stages of the S-curve, at least through proof-of-concept, most people did not understand the machine required to drive innovation. Innovation was so exciting that we immersed ourselves in innovating and lost track of the bigger picture: building the innovation machine that embeds innovation as a core competency. The I-pipe is one of the scaling mechanisms to ensure that innovation thrives. In fact, building the machine and making it work are what separate innovative companies from companies that innovate. It is the difference between continuous flow and batch.

I-pipes are common in makeup. They start with idea generation and move through stages to market launch. They often have common underlying principles: find ideas, test ideas, fund and build prototypes, experiment and get market feedback, scale up while reducing risk throughout production, and launch in the market. 3M continually ranks as one of the world's most innovative companies. Figure 5.1 is a simplified illustration of 3M's I-pipe.

The seven components of the 3M pipeline are as follows (Schneider, 2006):

1. *Idea screening:* ensures that ideas meet business screen
2. *Concept:* experimentation to prove concept has innovation potential
3. *Feasibility:* costing phase to determine cost to produce
4. *Development:* from concept to larger market test and greater funding requests
5. *Scale-up:* go-to-market plans and full funding requirements

Figure 5.1 3M's Innovation Pipeline

From the idea to the technical realization

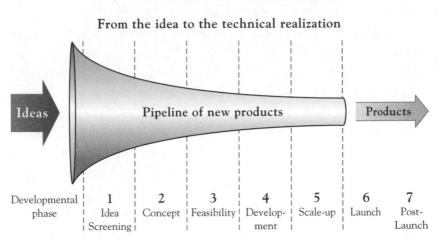

| Developmental phase | 1 Idea Screening | 2 Concept | 3 Feasibility | 4 Develop-ment | 5 Scale-up | 6 Launch | 7 Post-Launch |

6. *Launch*

7. *Post-launch:* focused on cost and quality of production and market execution

The Fantastic Voyage Through the Whirlpool I-Pipe

In process reengineering, it is common to "staple" oneself to a part and follow it through a factory to get a ground-level understanding of the manufacturing process. To understand the innovation process, we might staple ourselves to an idea. What follows is a best-case scenario of the way the innovation process would work in a perfect world.

The first phase of embedded innovation is an exploration process. It starts with a team that has an idea. With the help of an I-mentor facilitating the process, the team expands its idea to hundreds of new ideas and then groups these to create a large business space. The innovation team begins to converge down to a set of products, services, or business models. We focus on a set of products because one product alone can rarely create a sustained competitive advantage. One product can usually be copied, but a family of products is more difficult to duplicate— especially with a well-crafted migration path for upgrades and new rollouts.

Next, the team diverges by expanding their work again to select the best opportunity from the set of products, services, or business models. The team creates a migration path (a set of parallel but dependent paths with a series of related innovations over time) to meet its business objective and then the team completes a business plan. Next, the team conducts a self-assessment of its innovation against the Whirlpool definition of innovation. The innovation business plan and self-assessment are then prepared for an innovation review board (I-board) or other business team, which can opt to approve and resource the innovation. Embedded innovation creates an internal market-place of ideas with "buyers" and "sellers." In this open market for innovation, innovators often have to find a buyer. The I-pipe helps buyers and sellers find each other.

The composition of each I-board varies depending on the innovation; it can be a global product leadership team, a business or brand team, a senior leadership team, or a team of peers. Over time, innovation has changed so that all innovations do not have to go only through I-boards; business teams who have accountability for brands or product categories can also "buy" innovations.

If an I-board doesn't take the option, there are two avenues, short of killing the innovation, that the innovation team has at its disposal. One is to go back and improve the innovation to get a vote of approval from the I-board. The second option is to "sell" the innovation to another I-board or a business, which may invest.

Once the idea is accepted, it goes into the I-pipe for management and tracking. At the appropriate stages of development, the review board assigns resources: capital, talent, and other funding. Once in the I-pipe, the innovation is nurtured in its formative stages and rigorously tracked throughout its life.

Tollgate reviews occur at varying points in the I-pipe. At any point in the process, the review board can accelerate, slow, or shelve the innovation, or morph it into a bigger or different innovation. As the innovation progresses through the pipeline, it is scaled up and "de-risked" with experiments, leading to a launch decision. When the innovation launches, we track and report it in the innovation revenues, which are part of the overall operations revenues. Once in the marketplace, it grows to reach a steady state, at which point the next innovation from the I-pipe replaces it, creating a cadence of innovation that is hard for competitors to copy. In short, the I-pipe is the means by which ideas become innovations.

Making the Whirlpool I-Pipe Work

Although the basic processes involved in the I-pipe are straightforward enough, there are critical elements that have to be carefully aligned and structured to ensure that the I-pipe works well and produces real results. When we started innovation, Whirlpool spent most of its focus and resources on creating the innovations and moving them through the pipeline. We lost track of innovations once they hit the marketplace because our focus shifted to the next generation of innovations coming through the I-pipe. From 2004 to the present, Jeff Fettig's main focus has been to change that. As we mentioned in Chapter Four, he focused the company on extracting the value of innovations in the marketplace. He knew that if we did not keep tension on the post-launch process, innovation would starve due to the small results relative to the core, non-innovation results. The potential of our innovation process was almost lost in the "last three feet."

Figure 5.2 shows the Whirlpool I-pipe. Although most areas of the Whirlpool pipeline are similar to those in 3M's, our post-launch differs in our relentless focus on the innovation once a product is in the marketplace.

Figure 5.2 The Whirlpool I-Pipe

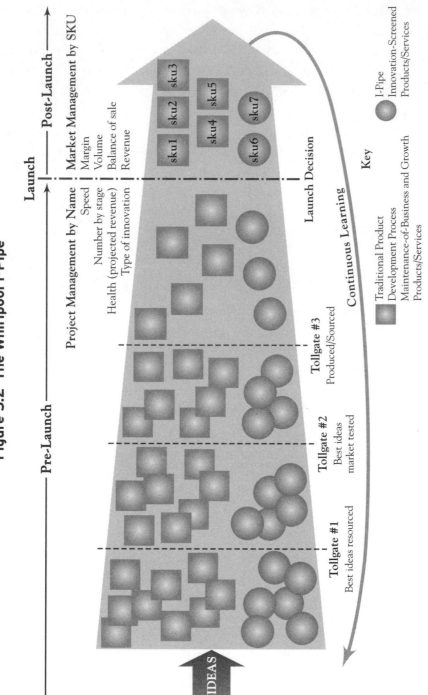

Pre-Launch

The pre-launch phase includes the fuzzy front end, the screening and calibration of ideas, and a series of tollgates that move ideas through the pipeline. Pre-launch has enjoyed a surge of attention in the last few years.

The Fuzzy Front End. The first step of the I-pipe is the fuzzy front end, so named because the ideas and concepts are unformed and untested. The trick to the fuzzy front end is not to kill ideas by requiring too much structure or financial certainty. The key is to limit the requirements and to establish a "dating service" that can join ideas from diverse sources.

The next sections look at some aspects of the fuzzy front end that are important for successful innovation.

The Idea Struggle. Many I-pipes start at idea generation and assume that ideas are easy to capture if you have the right net, but there is a step before you net ideas. Boeddrich (2004) reports on an inner struggle that an idea author undergoes before she vocalizes an idea. On one hand, the author is excited about the idea; on the other, she feels misgivings about putting the idea out into the environment, where both the idea and the author face an uncertain fate. Two key conditions reduce the idea struggle, Boeddrich says. First, a transparent, open, and fair process of idea generation and selection helps new idea authors see who had successfully contributed ideas. If the idea generation and selection process is random or discriminatory, then idea authors will continue to struggle—and many will hold back. Mariello (2007) also found that if the evaluation process for screening is transparent and standardized, employees would be more prone to submitting ideas. The second key condition to reduce idea struggle is a culture that accepts ideas from everyone. When a company starts up the S-curve, idea authors have nothing to rely on; they must take a leap of faith, trusting that their ideas will be welcome. To ease this difficulty, the company must quickly demonstrate that the concept of ideas from everyone is more than words by generating successful idea authors who become innovators.

How much should you resource the idea struggle and idea generation? Often companies get impatient with this stage and try to limit it or overstructure it. One way to think about this question comes from Boeddrich (2004). Ideas are one resource whose value appreciates with use: ideas gain value the more times they are used. Overcoming the idea struggle to get ideas into the fuzzy front end may be the most important, yet overlooked, section of the entire I-pipe.

Computer-Aided Idea Generation. One mechanism for overcoming the idea struggle is to use computer-aided idea generation. Computer-aided idea generation allows an innovator to put an idea on an Internet site and seek input from hundreds or thousands of people. For example, an innovator who wants to know how people use the space under their kitchen sink can put a survey or blog on an internal portal and ask this question to see if there is an innovation opportunity. Employees can respond and begin to build on each other's ideas. The innovator can host interactive chats about ideas he is developing. It is a good method for generating ideas from everyone. It is an inclusive way to start the fuzzy front end.

For embedded innovation, pairing computer-aided idea generation with skill building produces the best results. Computer-aided idea generation that becomes an electronic suggestion box does not build a capability. Collecting thousands of ideas for the I-pipe is important, but by adding capability building, computer-aided idea generation becomes a beacon to bring even more people into innovation. An example of adding capability would be to use computer-aided idea generation to start the process and then convene a group of the idea contributors to work together, with the help of an I-mentor, to advance the ideas beyond mere suggestions. As a result, the idea contributors would build an

ideation capability. The next example shows how idea generation can build a capability.

Voice of the Customer. Whirlpool has developed a process
and set of tools which ensure that the voice of the customer is
guiding the innovations on the front end. Although the other
innovation tools promote innovation, we found that there were
too few that forced data about customers into the innovation
process. As a result, innovations were not meeting the first criterion, that of being unique and compelling to the customer. The
area of customer insights, whether articulated or unarticulated
by the customer, is one that innovation architects constantly
need to enforce.

One tool, for example, that we developed helps innovators
determine customer benefit by taking them through a series of
routine questions about their target customer. Answering the
questions helps the innovators crystallize their innovation.
Voice-of-the-customer tools identify customer insights that
relate to the brand and ensure that the customer's voice is pre-
dominant in innovation. The tools force innovators to talk to
customers and make sure their voice is central to innovation.
They include a structured process for generating ideas and concepts fueled by the voice of consumers and by market trends, for
identifying consumer delighters and WOWs, and for helping us
work on the best ideas that serve our customers. They also provide feedback on the critical question, "Have we kept the brand
promise?"

Lens Smashing. Strategos created a brilliant process for generating ideas for the fuzzy front end: lens smashing. It begins
with adopting an expansive view of the world and gathering
new information by looking at the world through five lenses:
discontinuities, customer insights, economic engine, orthodoxies, and core competencies. The first three lenses are external;
the last two look at your company and what strengths you can

bring to the innovation. Discontinuities are trends in the world that innovators group together in a unique way. For example, juxtaposing the trend of nesting in the home with the higher incidence of diabetes in children could create a discontinuity that leads to a small, fun refrigerator to store insulin in game rooms for easier access. Customer insights are insights from customers either present or future. Economic engine looks at different business models for making money. Orthodoxies are paradigms or ingrained practices, the overturning of which creates opportunities. An example I gave earlier in the book was the orthodoxy that all our customers are women; overturning that Whirlpool orthodoxy led to Gladiator GarageWorks, a set of products and services targeted to men. Core competencies are the key parts of the company's business model that it does well. At Whirlpool, one of our core competencies is creating strategic partnerships with retail partners.

Teams first generate information in each of the lenses. They generally do this by dividing up and self-selecting the lens they care the most about. The subteams populate each lens with related ideas, then have a lens-smashing party. The information for each lens is put on hundreds of sticky notes, and then the team begins to assemble dissimilar information into strings of ideas by grouping sticky notes from different lenses. While the exercise smashes lenses together, what also get smashed together are diverse people who work on high-performing innovation teams to generate and evaluate their new ideas.

Lens smashing does what computer-aided idea generation does, but with two added components that are important for embedded innovation. First, from the onset it forces the innovators to learn new information by researching beyond their present idea set. (Succeeding rounds of computer-aided idea generation can do this as well, as people read and react to others' ideas, but lens smashing has this as a purposeful feature.) Second, lens smashing builds a skill set. Innovation teams learn to author ideas, work together, choose ideas, and take them to the next level. Usually, computer-aided idea generation relies on a host who screens ideas and moves the best ideas through the pipeline, possibly without any further involvement with the idea authors.

Lens smashing is just one way to fill the fuzzy front end with ideas. There are many tools on the market that help load the I-pipe with ideas. Open innovation models, such as P&G's Connect and Develop program (Huston and Sakkab, 2006), incorporate exemplary tools and processes to load the fuzzy front end. Embedded innovation favors tools that not only generate ideas but also teach innovation skill sets to the idea authors.

In the Whirlpool model, the fuzzy front end concludes with the screening of ideas, whereby, using the criteria derived from our innovation definition and the company's business needs, we decide which ideas will go forward.

Idea Screening to Qualify and Calibrate Ideas. There is abundant literature describing lessons learned on screening ideas for innovation. Here we focus on the lessons learned at Whirlpool. The first area of learning has to do with transparency of the screening and its importance to embedded innovation.

If ideas link to the company's strategy and if ideas transform into differentiated products through a structured system, innovations have a higher degree of success in the marketplace (Boeddrich, 2004). Whirlpool has a transparent and systematic screening process for ideas; first the innovation teams and then the sponsors screen the ideas. We screen, calibrate, and evaluate innovations against one another through a process called the I-box (Figure 5.3). Using a series of questions based on the three innovation criteria, the team rates their innovation. This process alone helps the team discuss how their innovation will fare in the marketplace. Once they work through the series of I-box questions, they calculate their response to determine a total score. The totals then transfer as a plot on the I-box. I-box questions address the innovation's

- Solution in meeting the customer's need
- Competition in the market

Figure 5.3 The Whirlpool I-Box Screening Tool

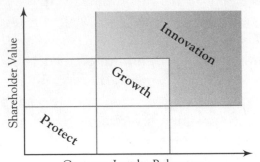

- Rigor of research or experimentation conducted to prove customer benefit
- Level of competitive advantage, from weak to dominant
- Net sales projections by percentage of incremental growth, margin, and economic value added (EVA)

The I-box is a tool that helps the team predict the performance of their innovation in terms of its relevance to customer loyalty and shareholder value.

It is important to note that an innovation idea must succeed on both the shareholder value and customer loyalty axes. The ranking assigns the innovation an overall score. The score classifies the proposed innovation as a protect-the-business idea (worth doing but not innovative), a growth project (makes money but is not innovative), and a true innovation that is both aligned with customer needs and values and promoting of shareholder value. If the idea is rated high enough on innovation, it progresses through the I-pipe. If not, it can still progress through product development, but is not counted as innovation. Thus the I-box process motivates innovators to adapt products that may start out as a maintenance-of-business requirement into innovation opportunities, providing an even greater benefit to customers.

The Innovation Factory: Converting Ideas to Results. The major part of the I-pipe converts screened ideas into innovative products, services, or business improvements. Converting ideas into innovations requires a large-scale effort to manage, group, test, resource, track, and improve them as they go through the I-pipe. We design the pipeline to scale ideas up to business launches while managing risk as we make greater investments. Some people at Whirlpool say that for every thousand ideas, only one will make it through the I-pipe. In actuality, once an idea meets the screening criteria, when others have been weeded out and the good ideas strengthened by the fuzzy front end innovation tools, more than 50 percent make it through the I-pipe.

To convert ideas to innovations requires a robust tool kit and process. In 2000, we licensed the Strategos tools and process. Since then we have added to the tool kit and dovetailed the processes into Whirlpool's business systems.

Idea conversion begins when we start scaling the idea through experimentation and testing it in the marketplace with consumers. We add resources while reducing the risk through increased knowledge and learning. The innovation passes through a series of tollgates designed to guide it through the process while continuously tracking and evaluating its business potential. At any point in the process, we can shelve innovations that do not fit our business needs. We report the I-pipe value and projected innovations quarterly to the EC. We also post the I-pipe online where any employee can view the pipe or any single innovation by product category or region, with varying degrees of security. For example, financial analysts can view the financial assumptions behind an innovation, whereas these data may not be available to others.

Post-Launch

Companies trying to embed innovation often overlook the post-launch stage. Many focus so heavily on their pipeline that they forget to put equal emphasis on their post-launch innovation in the marketplace. One company that finally came to grips with this problem realized that it did not "launch" innovations; rather, the innovations "escaped." Failure to monitor innovations carefully once they are in the marketplace usually means that the full value of the innovation will not be realized. In Chapter Four, we described how we reengineered our financial systems to track innovation results in the marketplace. Here we focus on value extraction.

In the market, customers determine the value of an innovation. Although many companies have post-launch metrics, many, including Whirlpool, failed to realize that the innovation process goes through post-launch until you kill or defrock the innovation. (As noted in Chapter Three, we track the innovations as long as they are growing at a specified rate and are delivering above-average returns in the marketplace. If they are not making this critical bar, we fix them or take them off the innovation list.)

Whirlpool struggled in this area until Jeff Fettig put emphasis on extracting the value of innovations in the marketplace. Post-launch includes the execution of the innovation and, over the course of the market life cycle, the continuous innovations in how to promote and sell the product until it is no longer considered innovative.

Fettig started first with a management systems approach. He changed the financials to isolate and focus on individual innovation products rather than on broad product categories whose average performance might hide poorly performing individual products. Because our strategy was to embed innovation in the fabric of the company, Fettig wanted core product innovations managed within the core business, not by a separate post-launch team, so he worked through the existing marketing and sales teams for the core business. He wanted to embed in the core business the post-launch skill of continuing to monitor innovations as long as they met the definition of innovation. To do that required some hand-holding and new approaches to innovations once they launched.

For example, an innovative product we introduced was Briva, the in-sink dishwasher that launched to rave reviews. Briva is a clever small dishwasher that sits in the half of your kitchen sink that you never use. It washes the dishes that usually sit in that side of the sink, eliminating the need to run your bigger dishwasher. Briva has a top-loading door that, when closed, adds additional counter space. We launched it with our regular trade partners, but early sales were slower than expected. Consumers loved the product but found that retrofitting it into an existing kitchen required more remodeling than they wanted to take on for a dishwasher. Consumers who were building a new home or moving into a new condo were more receptive to installing Briva. Retail, the largest of our existing products, was not the best channel for Briva.

Jeff's post-launch value extraction process forced the market managers to hold Briva up to the light of its original business projections. Once they did, they saw the significant potential that it was not achieving. When the marketing managers started to look for more suitable channels, they turned to the builder channel. They innovated the post-launch process but also rethought the point-of-sale processes, builder incentives, and line structuring to ensure that Briva met its full innovation potential post-launch. It may seem that a product this exciting and innovative would garner attention throughout its life cycle without Jeff or the innovation post-launch process pushing for greater results. In fact, Whirlpool, and many companies, lose focus of launched innovations. We spent more time on the I-pipe before launch. A value extraction process for launched innovation helped Whirlpool keep the focus on the innovation for as long as it met the innovation criteria, which includes post-launch.

The Leaky Pipeline

If you think about the pipeline from end to end as a profit mechanism, there are many points along its length where value can leak. The potential of an innovation idea can be lost as it goes through the pipeline, a deflation of value that often renders the innovation to the status quo. One way to address this is to be sure that the predicted value is visible to everyone who works on the innovation so that they can align their work to support the predicted results. Further, the process that Whirlpool put in place is designed to prevent leaks. The first point at which leaks can occur is getting the best ideas out of people's heads and into the pipeline. Embedded innovation creates an environment with a set of transparent processes so that idea authors can contribute their ideas. The second leakage point is in the generation of ideas. There are many methods to generate ideas; the ones that involve diverse teams and new information work best. The screening stage is the next potential area for leakage. Having an operational definition for determining what is in and what is out—a single definition that all innovation teams employ— is an important means of stopping leaks. In post-launch, value can leak when the innovation does not perform to its projected potential or, more commonly, when it is neglected in the marketplace. Tracking and reporting the performance of the innovation in the marketplace assist the marketing managers or the salesperson to help innovations achieve their expected results. A more overarching problem that can weaken the I-pipe as a whole is the failure to see it as an end-to-end system. Helping innovators who work on every step of the innovation see the whole picture can maximize value of the innovation.

Integrating the I-Pipe with Other Systems

There were many instances when we integrated innovation with legacy systems—or when legacy systems needed to adapt to innovation. One of the most significant examples was the reengineering of the product development process to include the I-pipe. When we introduced innovation, the product development process then in use was over a decade old and deeply ingrained. It had its own set of unchallenged, long-standing peripheral systems, or, as we say about Lake Michigan, it had its own weather system.

The following is a description of four points in time that tell the story of how we integrated the I-pipe and the product development process. Each description is accompanied by a corresponding facsimile of an original PowerPoint chart. These charts are artifacts that represent the merging of the two processes. They should be seen as a window into the reengineering that takes place behind the scenes to develop the right rational framework.

Product Development

Circa 1999. As we mentioned, the product development process was in place long before the I-pipe. It was an effective stage-gated product development process that served Whirlpool well. As Figure 5.4 shows, the stages were conceptualization, conversion, and execution, with tollgates between each stage. In this and more expanded versions, the product development process looks like a wiring diagram with squares, triangles, and arrows.

Figure 5.4 Product Development (c. 1999)

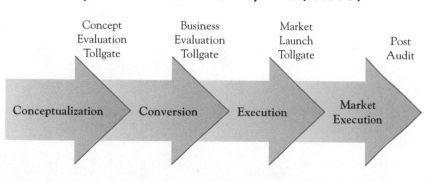

It's angular, black and white, and two-dimensional, with a strong engineering feel to it. There was some hint of customer insights in the conceptualization, but no hint of innovation.

I-Pipe

Circa 2000. The chart in Figure 5.5 depicts a zippy, upbeat process with a funnel that starts out large at the left of the chart and narrows as it traverses to the right. The phases are ideas, business case, experiments, prototype, and scale-up, overlaying the "double diamond" process of innovation through which ideas expand and converge at key decision points.

Product Development Meets I-Pipe

Circa 2001–2003. The product development and I-pipe processes now are on the same page, but separate, as shown in Figure 5.6. At this point they merely coexist on a document with a common appearance; they are not integrated in real life.

Figure 5.5 I-Pipe (c. 2000)

Double Diamond Innovation Process

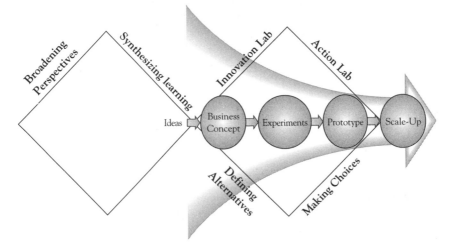

Figure 5.6 Product Development and I-Pipe (c. 2001-2003)

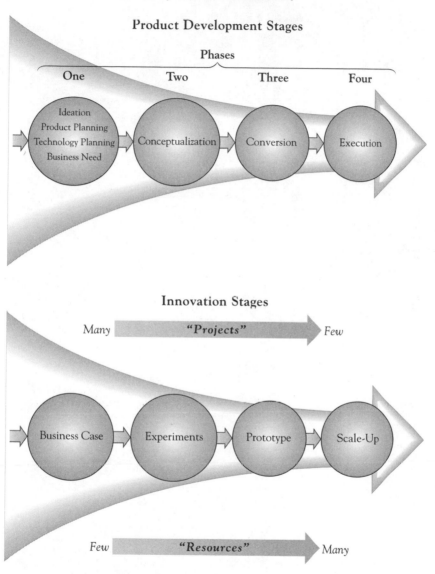

Product Development Stages

Phases

One   Two   Three   Four

Ideation
Product Planning
Technology Planning   Conceptualization   Conversion   Execution
Business Need

Innovation Stages

Many   "Projects"   Few

Business Case   Experiments   Prototype   Scale-Up

Few   "Resources"   Many

Figure 5.7 Product Development with I-Pipe (c. 2003)

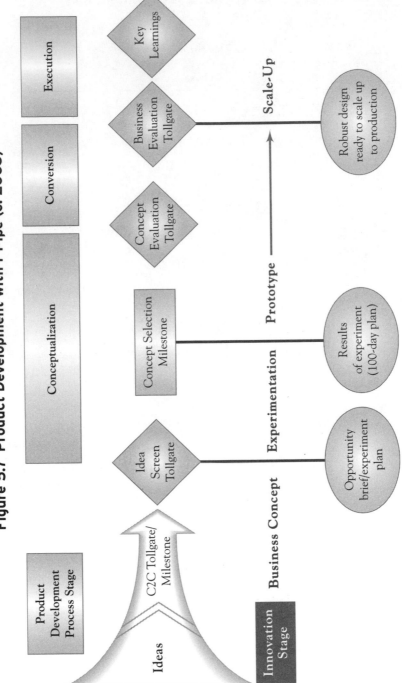

Can't Believe They Were Ever Separate

Circa 2003–present. The product development process and I-pipe are combined into the same model: victory at last. As shown in Figure 5.7, innovation and product development stages have common tollgates. The tollgates are derived from the best thinking of both innovation and product development: idea screen tollgate, concept selection milestone, concept evaluation tollgate, business evaluation tollgate, and key learnings milestone.

This is one story of reengineering and integrating systems to drive innovation. Imagine what occurred behind the scenes to achieve the integration.

The I-pipe is the machine the drives a continuous flow of innovation into the marketplace. As we have discussed, pre-launch activities include overcoming the idea struggle, generating ideas, screening, and converting ideas to innovations. Embedded innovation forces the innovation architect to continually adapt and correct the pipeline so that leakages do not occur. The strategic architecture, management systems, and the innovators themselves all work to ensure that the pipeline delivers maximum value. These innovators, who make it all possible, are the topic of the next chapter.

6

INNOVATORS AND
INNOVATION MENTORS

The future belongs to people who see possibilities
before they become obvious.

—Ted Levitt

Who can innovate? Whirlpool's vision of innovation from
everyone, everywhere is an inspiring but challenging one. Taken
literally, this phrase means that innovation can come from any of
the seventy-three thousand people working at Whirlpool throughout the world. Can this be true? Can anyone from a senior leader
to a person on the factory floor actually innovate and be taken
seriously? As the stories we present in this book demonstrate,
the answer is a resounding "Yes!" This chapter tells the story
of the people from all corners of Whirlpool who captured the
imagination, energy, and talent of an entire corporation in making
innovation from everyone and everywhere a reality. We begin by
describing how we selected and trained people in the innovation
process to facilitate and enable innovation across the company—
we call them I-mentors—and discuss what motivates them to take
on this role and the powerful impact it has had on their lives.
We then show how a critical mass of I-mentors can help create a
chain reaction of innovation, and end the chapter by examining
the reciprocal impact I-mentors have had on Whirlpool.

Feeding the Hunger

We knew intuitively that all people around the world are driven
to create something bigger than themselves. We believed that

this need to create, contribute, and find meaning is a fundamental human need that in being fulfilled could address both individuals' search for meaning in a large company and Whirlpool's search for innovation that would distinguish the company from its competitors. We knew that if we limited innovation to a select few, we would lose the incredible advantage of the energy, insight, and imagination of tens of thousands of people. Indeed, once we declared innovation as a core competency and announced the vision of innovation from everyone, everywhere, we were bombarded with ideas and requests from people who wanted "in." People who participated fell into three categories: individuals who were tasked specifically with innovation as a normal part of their ongoing product, service, marketing, customer experience, trade partner, or brand responsibilities; people who wanted to become I-mentors; and teams and individuals who were not part of either one of these groups but who had great ideas for innovations.

When we began, we really did not have a good idea about how we were going to bring our vision to life. We did know that we wanted to maximize the potential for anyone to innovate, that we did not want to stifle any idea, *and* that we had to innovate within our brand focus or risk eroding or destroying the advantage we had there. We decided to go with what had worked so well for our culture before: a dissemination approach that would allow many to operate in the innovation space within a structure of "soft guidance." This is the story of the people who innovated in that space.

The First Innovators

The first seventy-five innovators under our new vision were people drawn from around the world. They were the first group of people to work with our partner Strategos. Strategos' expertise is in teaching a set of concepts, tools, and methods—such as the lens smashing exercise discussed in Chapter Five—that foster innovation within a company. These included methods for generating ideas that can be leveraged into innovations, evaluating ideas, and experimenting with them to ensure that they are turned into innovations that are valued by customers.

These seventy-five individuals enjoyed almost rock star status—they were "officially" part of the new era in Whirlpool. They left their "real jobs" to move temporarily to one of the three regional headquarters to become "innovators." Their task was to learn innovation tools and methodology and then to disseminate the learning to the rest of the company. The idea was for twenty-five of the original seventy-five individuals to go back into the business to use the innovation tools in their daily work. The second twenty-five were to run business units that were started based on innovation results, and the third twenty-five were to teach others the tools and skills.

Twenty-five people were not enough to fill the demand of people and teams who wanted to learn innovation techniques. The good news was that we had created a need to innovate, and people and teams around the world were taking our vision seriously. The bad news was that we were totally unprepared for the level of demand—looking back, this was a good problem to have. To solve it, we decided to draw on what had worked so well in our company in the past, with an inclusive twist.

Building on Our Strengths

One of the reasons Whirlpool enjoyed a competitive advantage in a very tough industry in the last few decades was a strong focus on what we called operational excellence (OPEX). We had embedded this competency in the late 1990s, as well as an aggressive and cutting-edge Six Sigma program. Operational excellence was deeply embedded in the culture at Whirlpool, particularly in the manufacturing, technology, and engineering groups. Over one thousand people in these groups are certified black belts in Whirlpool's OPEX methods. These individuals not only took responsibility for conducting the projects to reduce variation; their sheer numbers had managed to change our culture. Individuals trained in these methods were zealots, and OPEX methods, measures, and practices were so deeply embedded that even if we wanted to undo the change in culture and de-emphasize operational excellence, we would not be able to do it.

People trained as black belts and master black belts in OPEX enjoyed a special status at Whirlpool, and although we did not want to create a set of elite innovators, we did want to school as many people as possible in innovation techniques so that they could not only innovate themselves but also mentor teams and individuals in the innovation process. With the help of Strategos, we created the skill set for I-mentors.

To date there are more than eleven hundred people trained as I-mentors. (Some of these I-mentors are also certified OPEX black belts.) Their backgrounds are varied—they come from engineering, manufacturing, technology, finance, human resources, accounting, and many other functional areas. This cross section of individuals fosters our vision for innovation from everyone and encourages innovation in all areas of the company, including business processes.

I-Mentor Selection and Training

In the initial stage of the innovation effort, people were nominated by their manager to become I-mentors, but the process quickly grew to include self-selected volunteers. It is important to note again that people who are selected or who volunteer for I-mentor training are from all disciplines and all levels in the company. We want to be certain that we are adhering to our vision of everyone, everywhere. Thus few restrictions were placed on people who wanted to become an I-mentor other than that the person have a good performance record and want to contribute to innovation. As the training progressed, we paid more attention to ensuring that there was diversity in each training class, including people from different functional backgrounds, tenure with the company, and years and type of experience.

To become an I-mentor, a person must attend a rigorous training program that outlines Whirlpool's innovation process, tools, and techniques. The training begins with three weeks of instruction in using the innovation tools. In addition, each I-mentor candidate is required to work on several innovation projects where he or she can apply the tools in real time. Only after the candidate has applied the tools and reported results on a real innovation project can he or she apply to become a certified I-mentor. Certification is a rigorous peer review process that evaluates the I-mentor's skills, application, and results.

The course content is broad and diverse. In addition to learning innovation techniques, I-mentors learn how to conduct a small market experiment to see if an innovation is viable as a business option, and to put together a brief for senior managers to decide whether or not to fund the innovation. The following are some of the highlights of the I-mentor training:

Linkage of innovation to other Whirlpool processes, such as product development. It is critical that Whirlpool employees understand how to align the innovation process with other critical systems within the corporation. Thus there is course content and material that focuses on alignment of business processes, such as finance, product development, and manufacturing, to the innovation process.

Developing customer insights, requirements, and benefits. I-mentors learn that customer insights as well as trends in customer behavior are fertile ground for creative ideas and innovation. This knowledge is critical, as Whirlpool's history reflects perhaps too much focus on features and engineering design that did not align to customer trends, insights, needs, or wants. Time is also spent learning about the voice-of-the-customer tools we discussed earlier, translating ideas into customer requirements for products, features, services, or the buying experience. I-mentors learn how to translate customer requirements into benefits that can be easily communicated and explained to the customer population.

Ideation and brainstorming techniques. I-mentors learn how to generate ideas using a variety of techniques and tools. Many of these tools are licensed from Strategos, but over the years we have added many new tools as needs arise. Most of the techniques seek to expand people's thinking about possibilities within the context of customer needs or wants. One of the most popular is called "breaking orthodoxies": innovators brainstorm "what people would never say" about a product or service and think about the orthodoxies or tacit assumptions that these unspoken ideas represent. I-mentor candidates then explore what would be possible if those orthodoxies were overturned.

Creating a migration path to a dream state. One of the most critical skills that I-mentors learn is how to create a migration path to a future dream state. Often a new innovative idea cannot be realized immediately, due to inadequate technology or resources, or for other reasons. I-mentors learn how to create a migration path necessary to make their idea a reality. This includes pinpointing "off-ramps" (decision points about the viability of the innovation project) along the way.

Experimentation and business model development. One of the critical elements of I-mentor training is creating a business plan for their innovation. I-mentors learn how to create a model of how their innovation will become profitable. This includes a plan for experimentation with their innovation to offer a proof of concept for the innovation and to refine the business model based on actual experience in the market.

I-Mentor Roles

I-mentors fill a variety of roles at Whirlpool. Most I-mentors are part-time, working full-time in other capacities. Many people who get certified go back to their business units and their jobs with an enhanced skill set that they use to foster innovation in their work unit.

Many I-mentors train other I-mentors and act as consultants to groups at Whirlpool that need an I-mentor to guide them through the innovation process. Business units or work groups tasked with innovation or who have found a new idea can request consultation and other assistance from I-mentors from the regional group charged with core competency embedment. An I-mentor may already be embedded in the group, or is assigned to facilitate and offer advice throughout the innovation process. This I-mentor works with the group to teach innovation skills, provide advice about the innovation process, and drive the innovation process; he or she might also bring in other experts in customer excellence or OPEX to create a robust approach to customer, product, service, or business process innovation.

Motivation to Become and Stay an I-Mentor

As part of the research for this book, we conducted a short survey of one hundred I-mentors to find out why they became an I-mentor and why they would take on such an assignment, considering that ninety-five out of the one hundred surveyed said that being an I-mentor was not their primary responsibility. Over 50 percent of the I-mentors surveyed gave the same six top reasons for becoming an I-mentor:

1. A chance to create and try new things
2. A workplace setting to think and create
3. A way to learn more about different parts of our business
4. A way to learn something new
5. A chance to meet and work with diverse people
6. A way to be included in something that is important to Whirlpool

It is interesting that these responses are so consistent. In fact, the top two answers, focused on creation, were cited by over 70 and 65 percent of the I-mentors, respectively. There were literally no answers that had to do with making money or getting paid more or anything remotely related to increasing the person's value within Whirlpool or in the marketplace. Interestingly enough, fewer than ten people mentioned that their boss's asking them to become an I-mentor had anything to do with their motivation.

When we asked people point-blank about why they would take on these extra responsibilities with no extra pay, these are some of the things we heard:

> "Money has nothing to do with this; you get richer from what you learn."
>
> "Well, I always thought 10 percent of earnings would be nice . . . but the excitement from working in a 'skunk-works' kind of environment beats the money aspect! It's fun to be an 'underdog' that no one expects to win."
>
> "Why not? It's not always about money! This gives me a chance to expand my thinking in a strategic way and help others do the same."
>
> "It is needed and helps me do my job. I don't see it as an extra role but as an extension of my particular job. It is something I am passionate about."

These quotes clearly illustrate that the energy, sense of belonging, and chance to learn and grow are major motivations to innovate—and show why the emotional drivers we discuss in Part Three are so important. Often managers believe that to motivate people to innovate, you have to pay them more or incentivize them in some way. What we learned during this process is that people, no matter what line of work they are engaged in, are motivated by learning and growth and the desire to be a part of something bigger than themselves. Although money is necessary, it does not by itself fulfill people's natural inclination to learn and grow.

We also asked our I-mentors what their most powerful experiences were in terms of capturing the spirit of innovation from everyone and everywhere. We found that people's answers fell into three main categories.

Enhancing personal life. We were surprised to find that many of the I-mentors mentioned that the innovation thought process, tools, and techniques had actually spilled over into their personal lives and changed the way they approach personal initiatives.

> "From my point of view, the goal is the happiness. All time we are looking by our happiness in a lot of different ways: professional, personal or familiar success, like person, husband, father, or son. This has contributed to my happiness at work and this has migrated to my personal life."

> "I have changed my personal life. Being exposed to a new mentality, I applied most of the new mental approach to my family life."

Fulfilling customer needs and desires. Another theme was the joy in contributing to fulfilling customers' needs and desires. The act of creating products or services that could contribute to customer satisfaction, joy, and loyalty was a recurring theme in people's responses.

> "When the innovation directly relates to a consumer need or desire . . . the ability to customize, organize, make it easier to use the product, etc."

> "The spirit of creating or identifying something new and as a consequence to be in some way a 'creator' of a new thing or a new product/service we can give to our customers in order to fulfill or satisfy their needs."

Using the tools in philanthropic or volunteer interests. The final theme was the use of innovation tools and techniques in volunteer or other related work outside Whirlpool. The Epilogue of this book tells stories of I-mentors who use the innovation tools and process in a volunteer capacity. Whirlpool encourages its employees to get involved in community-based volunteer work and to use what they learn at Whirlpool in these endeavors. About 35 percent of the people we talked with had actually used the tools and techniques they had learned during their I-mentor training.

> "I think about (even though I'm not aware of the details) the work program developed for women in Minnesota trying to create a new life for themselves via a trade. The innovation process helped create a work program for women to go become service technicians."

> "When I was working with a local non-profit, I used the tools to bring local government leaders to the same table to pool resources and share thinking . . . something never done before because of the lack of collaboration and fighting for the same resources."

Social Networking and Sustainable Innovation

One of the purposes of training as many people as possible in innovation skills was to foster social networks of innovators who could play off of one another and promote sustainable innovation that is part of the culture and the way of doing business: a critical mass of I-mentors would lead to a chain reaction of innovation.

As part of Leading the Whirlpool Enterprise (LWE), the leadership development initiative discussed in Chapter Four, we conducted social network analyses of two newly formed teams focused on the product development process, of which the I-pipe is a subset, to examine their social interactions to see if they were fostering sharing and cross-team fertilization of ideas and best practices.

Social network analysis is a methodology that looks at the self-reported interrelationships between team members and builds a map of the interactions based on a topic, in this case innovation around the product launch process. It is a picture of social capital or the frequency and type of relationships between team members and members of different teams. For innovation and the innovation launch process to be considered healthy, they should also produce interactions that are rich and robust and that have an appropriate amount of tension around new ideas and translating them into innovations that work in the marketplace. The underlying concept is that with common language and methodology, and a way to share learnings about innovation, innovators can actually build off of one another's ideas and, in the long run, create even more innovative solutions for customers.

One of the teams we examined focused on the first launch of new products; the other looked at the post-launch process. In the network maps shown in Figure 6.1, each dot represents a person, and the lines represent the relationship between the people. Each map can be analyzed by function, location, time with the company, or any demographic imaginable. (The maps in the figure do not have added demographics.) We asked each person to name the people with whom they interact on the topic, post-launch for example, and to rate the nature of the interaction, from good to strained. The longer the line between the dots, the more strained the relationship.

If you look at these from the standpoint of what should be occurring in product development, you see in the first-launch map a cluster of connected activity (on the left side of the map) with some satellites. The cluster is cross functional and healthy, although one must question what the satellites are doing. Contrast this with post-launch. Each cluster is cross functional and relatively healthy, but each cluster is an island; there are no bridges between clusters. It forces the question, "How are the best practices shared, and where are the learning mechanisms?" The post-launch team took this map and created a set of actions to build bridges and create a best practices network.

Figure 6.1 First Launch and Post-Launch
Social Networks (c. 2007)

First Launch

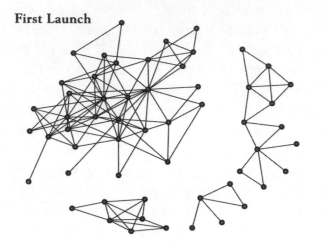

Example of new
product launch

Connected
central hub
with satellites

Post-Launch

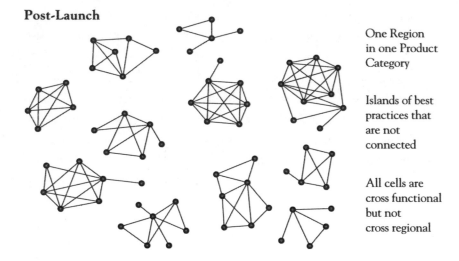

One Region
in one Product
Category

Islands of best
practices that
are not
connected

All cells are
cross functional
but not
cross regional

Burt (2004), a professor at the University of Chicago, writes on social network analysis. One of his findings is that managers who network across clusters are more likely to have good ideas because they have greater access to diverse or even contradictory information that they can use to create ideas with competitive advantage. He also notes that there is an import-export dimension for ideas, whereby an idea that one group perceives as average will be stellar in the eyes of another.

This led us to the notion that innovation should force diverse thinking across clusters by bringing them together to look for import-export ideas or for intersections between their diverse worlds. Social network analysis is a good tool to use to look at the effectiveness of innovation teams. It reminds us that innovation is not a one-time event, but rather a series of interactions, learnings, and progressions that innovation teams generate. We sought a way to foster this interaction naturally within the context of the innovation process and other Whirlpool systems and processes.

Whirlpool looks at the I-pipe as one of the mechanisms to foster the chain reaction of innovation. Innovators can use pre-launch activities, including overcoming the struggle for ideas, idea generation and creation, screening, and the process to convert ideas to innovations at every stage in the I-pipe, including post-launch. They also should be able to share lessons learned and best practices that make the next set of innovations more robust, creative, and customer focused.

The important point here is that simply having eleven hundred I-mentors on board does not guarantee the existence of the type of social networking and interaction necessary to sustain innovation. There must be structures and systems in place in the organization that "force" this interaction between innovation teams. Besides artificial means, such as conferences on lessons learned, having a structure in place for product, service, and customer experience launch teams to interact is critical to building the social networks necessary to grow and foster a culture of innovation.

Building a cadre of individuals who can contribute in a meaningful manner was critical to embedded innovation. However, what we learned is that the process, although far reaching and inclusive, could not be left to chance. Factors critical to the successful building of a cadre of innovators included making sure that (1) the process for growing innovators was in line with the culture and what had worked in the past for building cadres of people with skills (for example, the OPEX black belts described earlier); (2) the selection process really was inclusive, and the people who were selected were provided with the time and space to learn and apply new skills; (3) there was a structured training process that did not vary across regions and functions; (4) innovators were encouraged and allowed to use new skills back on the job or in other innovation roles; and (5) innovators were also free to apply their skills in ways outside of work that were meaningful to them and to the community.

The Innovators' Contribution to Whirlpool

When we launched the innovation effort, we imagined that I-mentors and other people involved in the innovation process would contribute to driving innovation and embedding it in the company, as well as to business results. What we did not foresee was the energy that people trained in innovation tools would bring to the company, their jobs, and the community. Indeed, there is something inherently motivating about creating and contributing to something bigger than ourselves. The I-mentor role and the roles of others trained and involved in the innovation process went beyond the educational and into the motivational, not because they acted as cheerleaders for innovation or the tools, but mostly because these individuals were so excited about contributing in an creative way to Whirlpool's success and, most likely, because they felt involved and engaged in making themselves, in some way, integral to the success of the company and the community. Including people from across the company in this effort created a widespread "energy field," the impact of which we could not have anticipated before we began our efforts.

Critically important as I-mentor energy and skills are, however, the energy and skills must be managed with discipline to ensure that innovation projects are executed in a way that produces results. This is the topic of the next chapter.

7

MANAGING EXECUTION
AND RESULTS

It's hard to be fully creative without structure and
constraint. Try to paint without a canvas.
—*David Allen*

A colleague of mine, Dr. Harry Davis of the University of
Chicago, talks about the underlying structure of jazz. It seems
counterintuitive that jazz has a structure. He describes it as "freedom with constraints." Although limits and structure seem antithetical to innovation, embedded innovation requires execution
that unleashes action and limits confusion but not creative chaos.

There is nothing unique about executing an innovation
plan; the same tools and skills for other initiatives work for
innovation. Many fear they will stifle innovation by instilling
rigor and discipline, but ideation and innovation management
are not the same thing. Ideation involves the idea struggle, idea
generating, and screening. This is the area where discipline and
too much process will stifle innovation, but ideation is only
one stage of the innovation process. Implementing the entire
embedded innovation process requires the same rigor and discipline that any strategic deployment requires.

In this chapter, we describe how the challenges of execution
evolve as a company ramps up the innovation effort and progresses along the S-curve; we also explore some of the confusion
surrounding innovation metrics and show how the S-curve can
be used to clarify which metrics matter when; finally, we discuss
the critical ingredient for successfully embedding innovation:
leadership.

Using the S-Curve as a Change Management Guide

Execution takes many forms. The S-curve is a predictive guide of the phases of execution, seen through the lens of organization change management. As discussed in Chapter Three, the S-curve is a six-phase model with a tipping point called breakthrough. The phases of the S-curve are launch, proof-of-concept, scaling, sustaining, value-creating results, and continuous improvement (see Figure 7.1). Change management disciplines often shy away from a push approach to change. The S-curve suggests that in the formative phases of embedding innovation, a push strategy is necessary. From launch to breakthrough, innovation is fragile and easily killed by the legacy systems and culture. There is a pull effect that starts early in the phases but is primary once you reach breakthrough. Embedded innovation needs both a push and pull strategy.

The model looks linear because we plotted the phases at the height of their dominance in embedded innovation. In reality,

Figure 7.1 The Embedded Innovation S-Curve

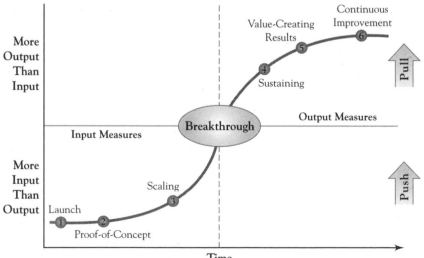

they overlap. We will look at phases 1 through 6 in detail, taking into consideration attributes that include objectives, problem set, activities, and potential sources of failure.

Phase 1: Launch

In phase 1, the senior leadership and the innovation architect mainly complete the work of discovery and planning. The objective is to create the strategic architecture and an embedment plan. The problem you are trying to solve is to select the innovation approach and align it with other business initiatives. This is also the time to ensure that you position embedded innovation properly within the overall strategy of your company. It is too soon to start deploying management systems or the I-pipe, or to begin working with the innovators. This phase is characterized by controlled chaos, and is a time to fight inertia or skepticism. In this phase, Whirlpool determined that we wanted innovation from everyone and everywhere, that innovation would be an enabler of an overarching customer loyalty strategy, and that our embedment plan would provide training for innovation teams whose members would go on to became I-mentors. The sources of failure in the launch phase include not approaching embedded innovation as a system (focusing on innovations themselves rather than on the processes and strategies that make them possible) and weak or disingenuous leadership. We will say more about the crucial role of leadership later in the chapter.

Phase 2: Proof-of-Concept

Phase 2, proof-of-concept, is the first test of the embedment plan. Here the approach and assumptions are put to the test to see if they will materialize the required results. In Whirlpool's case, we were testing the transfer of knowledge from Strategos to the first seventy-five innovators and to the innovation architects who were accountable for building the innovation machine. We were testing our everyone, everywhere approach by seeing if people from a broad cross section of the organization could use the tools to innovate. We were also testing the viability of the innovations in the marketplace. The objective of this phase is to delimit or pilot the approach to ensure success by limiting risk without overinvestment of resources. This may be a pilot; it is also a microcosm of the new innovation system you are trying to build. The problem you are trying to solve is to test the changes you plan to make to your rational framework. You are also trying to generate quick wins.

The characteristics of the proof-of-concept phase are dependency on the leader and some separation of the test from the rest of the organization so as to control and protect it. This phase is leader dependent because at this early phase only a few leaders are championing innovation. Innovation is still being "pushed" from the top at this point. Because in the early phases innovation is fragile, it is often tested outside the core or on a small area where learning can occur; then innovation can be scaled up to bigger and more risky areas or projects. However, you separate innovation while also holding a clear set of plans for how it is to migrate back into the mainstream of the business. Embedded innovation differs from a skunkworks because the main emphasis is on learning the capability and disseminating it. In this phase, you will start building your I-pipe. The more open and transparent this phase, the more excitement you will generate in people who are watching to see if this is real and going to last. Sources of failure in the proof-of-concept phase include poor design of experiment or a cookie-cutter approach that does not fit your environment.

Phase 3: Scaling

Scaling is the most difficult of all the phases—and the phase where most companies fail. The objective of scaling is to maximize future output and minimize current input. In embedded innovation, this translates to the successful involvement of thousands of people. The problem to be solved is how to leverage the tools and processes of innovation across the enterprise. The secondary problem is sustaining the initiative long enough to gain momentum without commensurate revenue results. This is where leadership patience is critical, as we explain later.

The key activities of this phase involve attacking the management systems and attracting innovators. There is a transition occurring from the few to the many, from the innovation architects to the leaders and then to the masses. You are creating scaling mechanisms to push you up the curve. In turn, leaders and groups start adapting the tools and process to fit their unique needs. Companies can go off track in this phase through "impatient" money, key leadership changes, or a halting of the initiative due to a business downturn before hitting breakthrough, the point at which innovation has a chance of sustaining itself.

In the middle of scaling you will hit breakthrough. Breakthrough is the tipping point. Results begin to occur. You start receiving external acknowledgment that boosts internal acknowledgment. You move from a push approach to a pull. Distributed champions abound throughout the enterprise. The results start compounding.

Phase 4: Sustaining

Sustaining is the next phase: making all the systems work to the highest state without allowing creeping complacency to slow down innovation. The objective is to ensure that innovation continues to thrive. It is the ideal point at which to add new types of innovations. At Whirlpool, for example, when we had a solid foundation of product and service innovation, we moved to adjacent businesses, new profit pools, and new businesses.

The twofold problem in this phase is to implement systems that promote financial rigor, so as to prove the results of embedded innovation while at the same time ensuring that those systems do not calcify and begin to stifle innovation with too many procedures, forms, and requirements. The characteristics of this phase include increased difficulty in tracking progress beyond the obvious metrics because innovation is embedded across such a large base. In this phase, innovation is self-sustaining, so leadership changes have little effect on it. Potential failure centers on complacency and believing your own press.

Phase 5: Value-Creating Results

The results of embedded innovation create a virtuous cycle: results engender more results. Innovation begets more innovation, and emotional drivers become self-generating as embedded innovation progresses. Other companies take notice, and new partnerships and opportunities present themselves. Financial success breeds financial success. Investors start to notice and add innovation results to their calculations, which lead them to have more confidence in the company and the leadership team. Customers begin to benefit from the innovation and are likely to pay more for it, increasing purchases while recommending the brand to their friends.

Phase 6: Continuous Improvement

Continuous improvement happens at every phase, but after a multiyear effort, phase 6 forces you to reevaluate the effort and determine what changes or overall improvements you need to make. Continuous improvement occurs at both the macro and micro levels. Evaluating progress and improving the metrics are important continuous improvement steps. The macro forces you to revisit the strategic architecture and embedment plan. The micro focuses attention on refreshing the components of innovation as new initiatives compound onto the enterprise. And because embedded innovation can grow complex and top-heavy over a number of years, in this phase you should look at how to continue to make the process easy and simple to understand.

Missteps in embedded innovation are hard to cover or hide because the base of involvement is so broad that everyone is watching. The best tactic is to admit you are learning and to treat the embedment process as one of discovery.

Embedded Innovation Metrics

According to a recent IBM study ("Expanding the Innovation Horizon," 2006) companies that are growing their profit margins faster than the competition are putting twice as much focus on business model innovation, as compared to companies that are underperformers in similar categories. Yet setting up the metrics that drive innovation are often a downfall of innovation efforts. Part of the difficulty lies in creating appropriate metrics for each phase of the S-curve. For example, in launch (phase 1), the metrics tend to be process metrics, as a measure of the organization's awareness of innovation. When you get to the scaling phase, then metrics related to results become key. An additional factor is that metrics are specific to each company and approach, making it harder to learn from best practices of other companies unless their approach is identical to yours.

A Boston Consulting Group (BCG) study (2006) asked participants how they use their innovation metrics. Most respondents use them to select ideas or increase return on investment in innovation projects; some use them for lessening time to market, ensuring R&D efficiency, and assessing the overall health of their pipeline. In our experience, the benefits of getting the metrics right include communication of the innovation process, marshalling support both from top leadership and from potential innovators, focusing resources on highest-priority areas, tracking and early detection of problems, and proving that the innovation process works.

Also, once you establish a baseline, you can use metrics, as Whirlpool does, to establish goals for improving the entire innovation process.

The 2006 BCG study on innovation metrics also found some startling results: companies generally undermeasure innovation, but even when they do measure it, they are not confident that they are measuring it properly. The ones that do measure innovation use an average of five metrics. In fact, there is a plethora of possible metrics to use for innovation. Confusion sets in when trying to pick the right metrics to use.

In the BCG study, the three metrics that were most commonly used were time to market, new product sales, and ROI of the innovation initiative itself. But there are many, many other metrics. Many companies adopt the famous 3M measure for innovation: the percentage of sales from new products launched over the past three years. Some companies move beyond sales to the harder-edged measure of operating margins; others use profitable growth, which includes both returns and invested capital. Linder's study of innovation measures (2006) includes process, growth, and profitable growth. She suggests using a portfolio of measures that capture profitability, are forward looking about competition, and include all types of innovation. Linder suggests using the following process measures:

- Idea inventories
- Employee engagement
- Resource allocation
- Share of widely cited patents
- Number of patent awards
- Milestone hit rate
- Speed to market
- Track record of individual innovators

Growth measures include the following:

- Share of wallet
- Growth in revenue
- Customer upgrade modeling

Linder cites growth in enterprise profits and margin premium as appropriate measures of profitable growth.

Additional metrics to consider include R&D spending, projected versus actual performance, customer adoption rate, total funds invested in growth projects, allocation of investment across projects, cannibalization of existing sales by new offerings, percentage of ideas funded, and number of projects killed.

It is no surprise that most companies use more output measures, looking at what comes out of their I-pipe, than input or process measures. BCG (2006) found that only 60 percent of its survey respondents have input measures, whereas 78 percent said they measure the output of innovation. However, many of the companies admitted they do a poor job of measuring the critical drivers of output performance.

With so many possible metrics to choose from, how do you select which ones to use? In our view, what you track depends on how far along you are in your innovation efforts—that is, your position on the S-curve.

Metrics and the S-Curve

In "Metrics for Innovation," Muller, Välikangas, and Merlyn (2005) suggest that selecting innovation metrics depends on whether your company is a beginner or a veteran in innovation. Their work coincides with our discussion of a company's progress through the S-curve. For companies that are beginning innovation, they list metrics by input, process, and output. For example, an input metric is the percentage of employees trained in innovation. A process metric would be the involvement of senior leaders in the innovation process, and an output metric would be the percentage of employees who can identify the innovation targets. Contrast this with the metrics used by veterans of innovation, such as Whirlpool. Our input measures include the number of I-mentors in the organization, process metrics include time to market, and output metrics include the number of strategic options by dollar value of new opportunities from the core business.

In summary, embedded innovation requires a set of metrics to track the progress of key areas of the business framework, which vary as the company moves along the S-curve. Table 7.1 shows one example of how the metrics align to the S-curve phases. Many of the metrics, such as employee engagement, can work well in more than one phase or can be carried to the next. Most metrics stay fairly constant, but take on a different characteristic as the company moves along the S-curve.

Table 7.1 Metrics for Embedded Innovation

S-Curve Phase	Commonly Used Metric	Whirlpool Example for Embedded Innovation
Launch	• Employee awareness of innovation initiative • Involvement of senior leaders	• Employee awareness of innovation initiative • Involvement of senior leaders • Adequacy of resourcing for approach • Level of agreement on approach
Proof-of-Concept	• Systems reengineered to drive innovation • Senior leader sponsorship • Employee engagement • Employee awareness of innovation • Customer impact • Percentage of ideas funded • Number of new external partners	• Number of I-mentors • Percentage of workforce trained • Key business systems reengineered • Employee engagement results • Number of ideas in pipeline • Number of shelved ideas • Revenue generated

Scaling

- Number of ideas in I-pipe
- Speed to market
- Number of new innovators joining
- Resources moved to innovation
- Number of I-mentors
- Percentage of employees trained
- Goal-setting efficacy
- Number of patents
- Price premium due to innovation versus comparable base
- Number of projects killed
- Innovation rate of new external partners

- Number of I-mentors contributing
- Employee engagement results
- Number of ideas and shelved ideas
- Revenue generated
- Revenue and projects by type of innovation
- Health of pipeline

Sustaining

- Percentage of sales of innovations over x years
- Resources generated from innovation
- Share of wallet
- Run rates of innovation
- Actual versus projected costs and revenue
- Number of widely cited patents
- Post-launch market performance
- Number of awards
- Growth in revenue
- Social responsibility and community impact
- Speed through pipeline
- Number of active I-mentors
- Innovation per employee, I-mentor
- Operating margins of innovation
- Number of strategic options from innovation

- Employee engagement results
- Number of ideas and shelved ideas
- Revenue generated
- Revenue and projects by type of innovation
- Post-launch value extraction
- Health of pipeline
- External operating profit of innovations
- I-pipe value

In *Payback*, Andrew and Sirkin (2006) propose a "cash curve" as a key innovation metric. The cash curve is a plot of the cumulative cash expended over the phases of the I-pipe from concept to post-launch. You can begin by using planned costs and then, as the project progresses, you can add the actual costs. The smart innovations are the ones that generate a positive cash flow sooner. The cash curve is especially helpful when you use it to get a longitudinal view of an innovation portfolio. Many companies compartmentalize costs and investments without looking at the cumulative resources invested across time and projects.

Forward-Looking Metrics

Metrics that track planned versus actual results are not the only metrics embedded innovation requires. Forward-looking metrics are equally important. An example is the revenue potential of the I-pipe. This measure helps determine how the size and scope of innovations in the I-pipe ensure that you have acceptable innovation coming out at a steady pace.

Once you have baseline performance for the end-to-end I-pipe over a two- to three-year period, you can set goals for increasing levels of innovation. This mature level of goal setting is part of the S-curve progression and cannot be accomplished earlier in the S-curve phases. To establish I-pipe goals correctly, Whirlpool starts with Christensen's question (2007): What job did you hire your I-pipe to do? In Whirlpool's case, the job we hired the I-pipe to do is to generate organic growth through new products and services and to build the skills to embed innovation as a core competency. With baseline financials, we set I-pipe goals based on the value of launched I-pipe innovations, starting at the end and working backwards. To do this, we make the following estimates based on our baseline experience with the I-pipe:

- I-pipe "breakage" from screening to launch—percentage of projects that do not make it through the pipeline, for whatever reason

- Average time in the I-pipe—speed-to-market estimates for projects, from screen to launch
- Average ramp-up time of innovation revenue once launched—time in the market to realize profit
- Percentage of revenue declassified each year—projects that no longer meet the definition of innovation
- Percentage of innovation revenue that is incremental
- Average margin improvement of innovation projects—how much margin is above the best comparison, if available; for example, a new innovative washer versus the present best washer in our product category portfolio

From these assumptions, we can set an overall innovation revenue goal and work our way back to how much we need in our I-pipe to meet our targets, as shown in Figure 7.2.

Figure 7.2 Establishing Value and Setting Goals for the I-Pipe

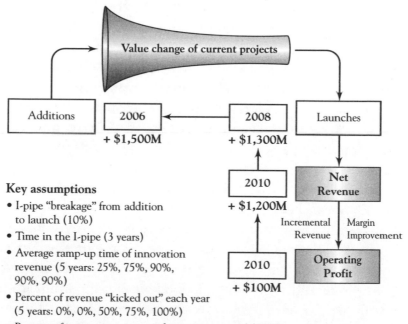

Value change of current projects

| Additions | 2006 | 2008 | Launches |
| | + $1,500M | + $1,300M | |

| | 2010 | Net Revenue |
| | + $1,200M | |

Incremental Revenue · Margin Improvement

| | 2010 | Operating Profit |
| | + $100M | |

Key assumptions
- I-pipe "breakage" from addition to launch (10%)
- Time in the I-pipe (3 years)
- Average ramp-up time of innovation revenue (5 years: 25%, 75%, 90%, 90%, 90%)
- Percent of revenue "kicked out" each year (5 years: 0%, 0%, 50%, 75%, 100%)
- Percent of innovation revenue that is incremental (40%)
- Average margin improvement of innovation projects (+2.5%)

The Role of Top Leadership

Wherever a company is on the S-curve, the role of leadership is critical to execution. The attitude of the senior leader and his or her approach to innovation make all the difference. There are no field books for leaders to read to know what to do to make innovation successful. In the next sections, we highlight three characteristics that are critical in leading embedded innovation.

Patient Money

Leaders need to adopt a long-term view when embedding innovation. In a sense, they need to take a leap of faith. In no area is this more obvious than in the investments made for embedded innovation. In the S-curve's phases preceding the breakthrough point, the organization is putting in exponentially more resources than it is getting out. If leaders adopt a short-term ROI mind-set regarding innovation, they might become impatient and stop innovation too soon. At Whirlpool, when Dave Whitwam set out the vision of innovation from everyone and everywhere and told us we would be successful when every job at Whirlpool had changed, it was clear that we were embarking on a long journey. As we noted in Chapter One, he wanted to develop innovation as a core competency at Whirlpool. He, and then Jeff Fettig, kept their eyes on that prize and never faltered.

3M uses a term that fits with the metrics conundrum for innovation: *patient money*. According to 3M's Web site, in 1904, Lucius Ordway introduced the term "patient money" and saved the company. Patient money is required when an innovation has promise but the numbers are not yet supporting the promise. It represents the long view of the innovation. 3M still uses the term to slow down the trigger finger of financial assassins who want to cut innovations before they realize their full potential. How patient is your investor's money? Part of the answer lies in your ability to establish good metrics that credibly measure the current state and can be used to set goals for the future state. Part of it also lies in the leader's ability, as Dave Whitwam put it, to look out the window and dream. Jeff Fettig is clear to point out that of course patient money has to lead to *money;* this can't be a question of patient money versus no money.

Withstanding Leadership Change

Constancy of purpose in embedded innovation is an important concept. Sometimes you have to let leaders experience the effects of not having it before they can learn how important it is. In 2003, one year before Dave Whitwam retired, the European business was under enormous pressure and faced a daunting year. The head of Whirlpool Europe at the time was Mike Todman, today the president of Whirlpool North America and a member of the board of directors.

In summer 2003, the European business had suffered a stressful six months. Mike was doing everything possible to streamline the business and get the European organization to have a laser focus on the marketplace. The day-to-day challenges were testing his people's resolve; it seemed there was not enough time to focus on the long-term innovation execution. They were in a fight for their life. After much deliberation, Mike decided to put innovation on hold. Just like that, he stopped all activities around embedding innovation. Doing so made sense; there were no innovation results coming out of the pipeline that would help him solve his daily pressures. He was not stopping innovation permanently, just putting it on hold with every intention of starting it up once the business turned around.

I heard Mike talk about this decision two years after he made it. His reflections on what happened were both chilling and inspirational. He was speaking at a senior leadership development workshop, and he told the group of assembled leaders that he had made the biggest mistake of his career when he put innovation on hold. He said that he did not understand at the time that the best way out of his daily business pressures was to keep innovation going.

It was not the revenue coming out of the pipeline but rather the mind-set, the emotional drivers that embedded innovation engenders, that could have changed his day-to-day business results. What he came to realize was that when he stopped innovation, he "killed the hope" of the people of Whirlpool Europe. Mike's prophetic message is an important lesson to senior leaders and innovation architects. Putting innovation on hold, even for a short time, diminishes the emotional drivers that are helping you in other parts of your business, as we discuss in Part Three. Emotional drivers unleashed by embedded innovation migrate across the business. Embedded innovation allows emotional drivers to surface and flourish. However, they have a half-life when you change direction or put innovation on hold. When you diminish emotional drivers, you create a hole you have to dig your way out of. You create a flavor-of-the-month mentality. Mike went on to describe to the leaders how long it took to regain the momentum lost through his well-meaning but detrimental decision to halt his efforts to embed innovation.

There is a shadow S-curve that takes over when you drastically change direction in embedded innovation. If you were working with a few of the top geniuses, it would only affect a few, but disruptive changes to embedded innovation affect everyone. They override your S-curve trajectory and draw a shadow S-curve that is much steeper, if you can regain the momentum at all. Mike was able to regain momentum because of the honest and brave public reflection he made about his hard lesson learned. Today Whirlpool Europe is one of the thought leaders in innovation at Whirlpool.

Thinking Strategically

CEOs have a unique perspective of the entire enterprise and strategy. Recently a CEO from a global company came to Whirlpool to learn about how Whirlpool embedded innovation. Jeff Fettig coached the CEO on how he could start innovation, how it could fit with other key initiatives, what the timing would look like, and how to find some quick wins.

As the CEO listened to Jeff talk about embedded innovation, he disclosed that he had launched a massive cost containment initiative the previous year that was not transparent to the people of his company and taking up all of his company's bandwidth. In hindsight, he realized he had made a mistake by not making the cost initiative open and transparent. He decided to delay the public start of the innovation effort until after his cost initiative reached its breakthrough. He knew introducing innovation now would overwhelm the company, but he decided that he and his top team could begin designing the strategic architecture and embedment plan. He vowed he would not make the same mistake with the innovation effort as he had with the cost containment drive. In fact, he talked about locating the start-up innovation team in the most central and open part of the building so that everyone could see what they were doing. As the meeting continued, he hammered Jeff with questions about investment, types of innovations, I-mentors, and the infrastructure of innovation.

He also posited that his company's prolific intellectual property campaign might hurt the start-up of innovation because the company rewarded scientists and engineers for all patents, of which only a third had commercial potential. He started to consider how to adapt this rewards system to enable embedded innovation.

We could tell by the depth of his thinking and commitment that this CEO was serious about innovation and that he had a good chance of being successful. He was thinking about embedded innovation at the strategic level and as a system.

Beyond Execution

Innovation is unique, but the way you execute it is not. The same rigor, discipline, and thought leadership are required to drive embedded innovation as are required to conduct other strategic initiatives. In that sense, innovation is rather pedestrian. Execution through metrics, value extraction, leadership, and S-curve change management will generate success in embedding innovation—so long as the emotional drivers that are already present in people are allowed to come out.

Although the design of the innovation machine is critical, the machine by itself can't do much without the buy-in and emotional investment of people throughout the company. The emotional drivers—learn, dream, create, heroes, and spirit—are critical to bringing the innovation machine to life. These are discussed in the next part of this book.

Part Three

EMOTIONAL DRIVERS

8

LEARN

Learning is what most adults will do for a living in
the 21st century.

—S. J. Perelman

The rational framework is critical for making innovation possible
and for ensuring that it aligns with business goals. But by itself,
the framework does not produce innovation. As we noted in
Chapter Two, new ideas and breakthrough results are created
not by frameworks or systems, but by people who dare to dream,
learn, and create—which is why the emotional drivers are so
important. We did not set out on our quest to embed innovation
at Whirlpool with these drivers in mind. We discovered them
along the way, and crystallized our thinking about them in the
process of writing this book. In this part of the book, we describe
these drivers and explain how they can be unleashed throughout
the organization to propel innovation. The first emotional driver
we discuss is our inborn human desire to learn and the enjoy-
ment we take in learning.

Innovation and learning are indelibly connected. Harkema
(2003), for example, defines innovation as the "mentality that
expresses itself through learning." Learning is one of the prominent emotional drivers that sit just below waterline waiting to
be unleashed. We found that vast numbers of people come
to innovation to satisfy the need to grow, and to aid their
company. Unfortunately, however, the norms of organizational
life—even at Whirlpool—often stifle learning. If you want
innovation to flourish, you must first make it clear to all that
they have *permission* to learn.

Permission to Learn

We work with many teams, both in Whirlpool and other companies, to develop skills and processes to implement their business plans. It is amazing how many of the teams are waiting for permission to learn and act. Feeling that one needs permission to act is itself a learned behavior. Perhaps it is from decades of command-and-control management practices. One team that we worked with used the metaphor of going out on the ice. The vivid picture of testing the ice and the possibility of falling through tells us how far companies have unknowingly gone to limit risk taking and learning.

Much of the work we do involves getting a senior leader to have a dialogue with a team and to say, "You have my permission to act. There will be failures and that is OK. Learning is part of the process." Helping teams that are stuck may look complicated, but the value added we bring oftentimes is simply getting senior leaders to tell teams that they have permission to learn and act.

To embed innovation—to seek innovation from everywhere and everyone—means granting blanket permission to act. Leaders need to find many ways to give permission to learners. Organizations need to remove the risk from putting ideas out into the environment—help people surmount the idea struggle we described in Chapter Five—by providing a skill set that builds confidence and by surrounding idea originators with a network of supportive people.

People's need for permission to learn and act is a barrier to innovation that can be removed through a rational framework and by unleashing the emotional drivers of embedded innovation. Once there are some successes and failures and nothing bad happens, learning begins to spread. Even those who are not "power-learners" get involved. The risk of failure or embarrassment is diminished and people feel freer to learn. Most important, this learning is occurring "on the ground," around key business needs, not in a classroom. The organization becomes unfrozen. Innovation leaders who keep the environment open and conducive to learning help embed innovation.

Embedded innovation moves innovators' learning from passive reception to active inquiry and testing. Innovators begin to control their destiny and to question everything. Motivated innovators who no longer need permission to act can threaten some senior leadership teams. However, in the new era of innovation and global competitiveness, leaders need to realize that to move quickly requires an engaged and driven group of people who do not have to wait to be told to act. The trade-off should be an easy one. Embedded innovation changes everything, and leaders become better leaders by establishing a sandbox and the skill set, removing barriers, and then getting out of the way and letting the magic happen. Leaders should understand that companies with embedded innovation are learning organizations that are hard for competitors to copy. Companies that unleash the potential of innovators who have a passion and aptitude to learn and act on their own will be the companies who remain competitive. The rest will fall behind.

How the I-Pipe Enables Learning

The emotional driver of learning is a strong magnet that pulls many people into the innovation process. Embedded innovation offers a new and exciting learning process. To demonstrate the learning that occurs, we follow the innovation process, focusing on how innovators are learning throughout I-pipe. Figure 8.1 depicts the I-pipe stages at the bottom of the chart and the learning phases A through C at the top. Imagine an entire organization learning the skills described in the figure.

Phases I to II: Insights to Ideas—Expansive Thinking

At the start of the process, the innovators are collecting insights about the marketplace through research and interactions with

Figure 8.1 Embedded Innovation Learning Phases A Through C

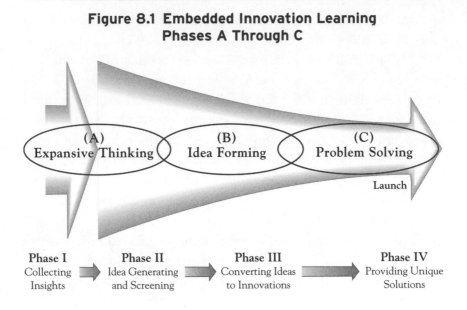

others. Examples include demographic changes, disruptive technologies that are emerging, health changes, or changes in the home over the next decade. From the insights, the innovators go through an idea generating and screening process. Collecting and creating insights in the idea generating phase is an expansive learning experience. In these early phases, innovators are seeing information through new eyes.

The process is inductive and chaotic, and the learning is divergent and expansive; the process tends to be fun and exciting. In this early phase, the hard work of innovation has yet to begin. The experience is enlightening and intellectually challenging at the same time. Innovators are looking to the future in unbounded ways, creating possibilities. There is white space to be discovered.

During these early phases, innovators are learning the skills needed for the social networking that occurs in embedded innovation. Diverse teams learn a common set of tools and language. The power of this learning is extraordinary. This phase begins a subtle change in the mind-set of innovators. As they work across different boundaries and with new people, they adopt new perspectives and expand their thinking. They begin to gain a sense of how the business works and what it takes to be competitive. They develop a bigger view of the world, a view that was once found only at the top of the organization.

I-mentors play an important role in facilitating this learning. Taking innovation teams through the collecting of insights is a great experience for I-mentors. They are teaching the tools and process and are helping others learn. For many I-mentors, this is the reason they joined innovation in the first place: to learn and teach. Many of them say they like seeing the "shining eyes" of people as they start to see the possibilities (Zander and Zander, 2001).

Phases II to III: Ideas to Innovations—Idea Forming

In these phases, the focus is on selecting which ideas to pursue. This is where the hard work of innovation kicks in and where, if you are not passionate about your idea, you can end up watching the clock. This is hard work, but it is also satisfying. Embedded innovation has a freedom to it that allows many innovators to vote with their feet.

This learning phase teaches innovators to form an idea for an innovative product, service, or business model. Idea forming includes transforming a set of fuzzy ideas into a specific concept. Learning in this phase relates to converging on an idea, decision making, and risk taking. The learning becomes more intense around the social interactions of team decision making. Innovators learn the right questions to ask and the selection mechanisms to narrow their ideas to a preferred choice. This phase includes creating a picture or an elevator speech so that the team can sell its idea to potential evaluators and investors. Learning to sell an idea is a coveted skill, no matter what job one has.

I-mentors are valued in this phase. This learning phase tends to be less chaotic, but innovation teams still look to I-mentors for guidance. Seasoned I-mentors help teams by providing examples and best practices from other innovation teams. They become a knowledge transfer mechanism. They use the tools and their expertise to help clear the hurdles of decision making and risk taking. I-mentors help teams build confidence because they have been through similar experiences. If you sit and observe this phase of the process, you can see learning happening in front of your eyes.

Phases III to IV: Innovations to Solutions—Problem Solving

These phases take the innovation to market. This is where all the hard work is tested—the innovation works or it doesn't. This phase may add team members who specialize in go-to-market skills.

Innovative teams change in membership over time. As the innovation progresses through the I-pipe, new and more specialized innovators join the process. Without an overall system of shared process and language, adding new members could be disruptive. When there is such a system, new members can improve the innovation by bringing fresh perspectives. This phase takes even more hard work; the team spends grueling hours converting the idea into a prototype and conducting experiments to test the innovation. It involves learning how to attract more resources—people, funds, and capital. It can also involve realizing that the innovation is not going to work and making the tough call to shelve it; doing so can often provide valuable lessons that can be applied to future projects.

In this phase, innovators are learning how to solve the problems that emerge as the idea is put to the test and as their team gets feedback from customers. Teams learn to develop tenacity and toughness, a doggedness about their innovation. They learn to discern which kinds of feedback are valuable and which are not.

In this phase, the I-mentors teach innovation teams how to design marketplace experiments and how to interpret the results. Often the I-mentors are teaching innovation tools that help the team problem-solve. These tools have to do with customer insight, the economic engine, evolution, and preparation for I-pipe tollgates.

Learning Enables Change

One of challenges companies face today is the rate of change they are experiencing. CEOs routinely rank it as one of their top concerns. There are many books and articles on change and how to get organizations to be change ready. One trait of learning, according to Basadur and Gelade (2006), is that it makes the strange familiar. Embedded innovation creates an atmosphere of change that makes the strange familiar, even valued, because to innovate, people look for strange and unique intersections among ideas.

Creating a learning organization is creating a organization that can change. Innovation drives both new thought and action. According to Vera and Crossan (2004), and partially based on Crossan's earlier work, the basic paradox of organizational learning is resolving the tension between new knowledge and institutional knowledge. These authors present a model of learning that includes intuiting, interpreting, integrating, and institutionalizing. The I-pipe uses each of these processes, starting with intuiting in the idea struggle, during which idea authors move their insight to the innovation team through interpretation. As the team integrates noncontiguous ideas into an idea flow, they extrapolate or connect the idea to other ideas in the migration path. Finally, institutionalizing takes place in the I-pipe as the team embeds and progresses the idea through the I-pipe's structures, routines, and practices to become an innovation. Embedded innovation creates a learning organization with a sense of urgency.

The change that embedded innovation enables is self-initiated. In traditional change initiatives, executives or managers usually start the change and then force it on employees. Change management disciplines even use the term "target" to describe the person or group they are trying to change. In embedded innovation, people at all levels have the freedom to create change. The locus of the change shifts to the innovator. Learning how to create change is a valuable component to innovation, but selling the change is also important. Innovation teaches teams to create and sell change in the form of a product or service.

How Learning Connects with Other Emotional Drivers

As we have mentioned earlier, all the emotional drivers are connected, as illustrated in Figure 8.2. Learning connects to dreaming because dreams are secondary sources of insights that accelerate learning. Creating and learning interact powerfully when innovators learn tools and processes that enable them to turn creative passion into commercial innovations. The hero's journey is one of learning and growing. Finally, learning is a critical aspect of creating a spirit for innovation that in turn drives a learning organization.

Embedded innovation presents innovators and I-mentors with a unique learning opportunity. Although the walls of the innovation sandbox (Whirlpool's strict criteria for innovation) bound the scope of innovation, they do not limit the scope of learning. On the contrary, embedded innovation offers several kinds of learning: learning the innovation process and tools; learning the skills needed as an innovation moves through the I-pipe, as discussed earlier—social networking, selling, decision making, problem solving, and more; and learning about trends and concepts that lead to innovative solutions.

This third kind of learning is unbounded and amorphous. *What geopolitical or economic trends are emerging in the*

Figure 8.2 Intersections of Emotional Drivers of Embedded Innovation: Learn

	Dream	Create	Heroes	Spirit
Learn	• Accelerating learning through dreams • Learning to use dreams	• Creating new knowledge • Learning valuable and fun tools	• Fulfilling a journey of self-discovery • Forming ideas and problem solving	• Creating a learning organization
Dream		• Dreaming of possibilities	• Fulfilling dream of new identity • Following dreams to self-fulfillment	• Creating esprit de corps through group dreams
Create			• Unlocking creativity • Creating more heroes	• Engaging and attracting potential innovators
Heroes				• Revitalizing the organization • Creating mythology and cultural norms

world? What is changing in the home? How are people living and working? What demographic changes are predicted over the next twenty years? What problems are my customers trying to solve? As these questions demonstrate, innovation, by its nature, can expose people to interesting insights or facts about the world. Whereas learning about tools and skills is process learning, this third type is content learning. For many innovators, this type is unfettered. Some of it occurs through lens smashing, as described in Chapter Five. It gives innovators the opportunity to learn about trends, customers, the industry, and ways to make money.

Embedded innovation learning involves both acquiring and creating knowledge. It advances learning through a process of rich interactions that produce valued insights. Much of the new knowledge is generated through social networks. In traditional innovation models where only a few innovate, the rest of the organization may be aware of the innovation, but the only ones learning are the few privileged innovators or individual geniuses. Embedded innovation provides action-learning for a larger percentage of people in the company and an outlet for applying the learning to real business problems. At its best, embedded innovation creates collective genius.

What Motivates Learners

Potential innovators have a basic and insatiable need to learn. Embedded innovation removes the barriers to attraction and creates an open market for people who value learning. Of course, learning does not motivate everyone, but for those who are motivated, embedded innovation offers a level of learning that is hard to find in many jobs or other corporate initiatives.

Watch children play. They have a natural curiosity and oftentimes test the waters without thinking through the consequences. Children learn by experimentation and by repetition. They do not go through the deep thinking and reflection that adults require in order to learn. The motivation to learn is different in adults. According to Leib (1991) and based on Knowles's seminal work, there are six factors of motivation in adult learning:

1. Social relationships: to be in a network of acquaintances with a common goal
2. External expectations: to meet the increasing needs of the company or to work on meaningful initiatives
3. Personal advancement: personal competitiveness or ambition
4. Escape or stimulation: to break the monotony or routine of daily life

5. Cognitive interest: to learn for the sake of learning and to satisfy an inquisitive mind

6. Social welfare: to develop skills to help others or to serve the community

Embedded innovation meets all these needs. First, innovation is a team activity; the diverse thinking of team members and social networks creates a stimulating learning environment that inspires innovators. Second, many innovators at Whirlpool say that what they get out of innovation is a chance to help the company and to work on something important. Third, innovators understand that the skill set they gain through innovation creates personal competitiveness both inside and outside Whirlpool. Fourth, some jobs can be routine, even boring, but innovation is rarely either. Innovation provides an escape from monotony. Many innovators have told us they joined Whirlpool's innovation effort to add interest and variety to their otherwise tedious job. Fifth, innovation is stimulating. The expansive nature of innovation satisfies the inquisitive minds of many people who value learning.

The sixth factor is serendipitous. As we've mentioned elsewhere, the innovation process motivates many innovators beyond the company's four walls and provides a way for them to become socially responsible citizens. The Epilogue presents examples of this social responsibility and volunteerism coming from the innovators; it tells stories of innovation heroes who use the tools in their volunteer lives outside Whirlpool.

Adults learn by doing. Most traditional adult learning models include the following steps: do it, reflect on it, get new information about it, and apply it (repeat). Adult learning uses a problem-solving model. Embedded innovation starts one step before problem solving; it starts with forming or creating the problem. This added learning step is what makes learning in embedded innovation so powerful. When you are forming the problem, there are learning sparks—the proverbial "aha" followed by "WOW." Those sparks make the learning addictive. It attracts people. Often they can't get the "aha" drug in any other part of their work or even in their life. Embedded innovation makes this drug available to everyone, not the few. Learning is a key emotional driver to embedded innovation, in which even the learning is unique. Imagine an organization that is creating learning sparks and generating innovations as a result.

Organizational Learning and the S-Curve

Learning in embedded innovation is not confined to the individual; organizational learning is also stimulated. The nature of organizational learning changes over the course of the S-curve. In the launch phase, there is limited opportunity for learning, although there is awareness building. The organizational learning starts toward the end of the proof-of-concept phase, but it is during the scaling phase that organizational learning gains momentum. Scaling requires an efficient learning protocol to reach increasing numbers of innovators. By definition, this protocol involves knowledge transfer from one innovation team to the next. In addition, the ideas that succeed or fail generate significant learnings about what works and what does not. Organizational learning expands as companies progress up the S-curve. At the breakthrough phase, learning should be generating a payback and building a future platform for quicker execution of innovations. Once innovation reaches the sustaining phase, the organizational learning explodes into new areas. Future innovation teams can apply old insights to new spaces. The company is developing a learning platform that embedded innovation uses to move into new areas of innovation. For example, at Whirlpool we started with incremental core innovations of products and services. Once we had built our innovation learning platform, we migrated to adjacent businesses and new profit pools.

Building Learning into the Innovation Process

Innovation architects play a key role in creating a learning organization. In considering any proposed process or procedure, they need to apply a key rule of thumb, asking, *Will it build a capability? Will the organization create learnings from the process or tool that it will then apply to the next set of problems? Does the new element force the organization to think?* If only a few people are learning, the organization is not thinking. As innovation architects are building and sustaining the innovation process, they should screen each new embedment feature using a set of learning criteria. Here are three learning criteria, where X represents an added feature (such as computer-aided idea generation) to the innovation process:

- Will X bring new knowledge or new applications of existing knowledge?
- Will X be sustainable as a learning mechanism, or is it a one-shot deal?
- How can we reinvent X to add learning to it?

Computer-aided idea generation is a good example of an embedment feature. By itself, it amounts to a sophisticated suggestion box. What learning occurs for the idea authors who submit their ideas to the online gods? However, using the learning criteria, innovation architects can design a process to add learning to computer-aided idea generation. For example, the idea authors could screen the ideas if the screening definitions were transparent and shared. That would teach idea authors which ideas have the best chance of success or how ideas can merge to ensure that they have a chance at selection. Second, as a contributed idea gains traction, it can draw people together to refine and embellish it. In this way, computer-aided idea generation is the first step in a continuous learning process.

Embedded innovation enhances the process of creating a learning organization. The more people involved the better. An important feature of a learning organization is the latent learning that is stored and reused. If you think of knowledge as an asset, embedded innovation creates and stores knowledge for future innovators. The best learning organizations both generate and capture knowledge at an accelerated rate. In a perfect innovation process, ideas that do not become innovations are retained, and future innovation teams reshuffle them into new innovations.

It is easy to miss the opportunity to build a capability. Often we sell out the long term in favor of the short term. If the innovation architects are not helping the organization strive for building a capability, such a capability will not naturally occur. Adapting and repeating innovations can lead to organizational learning. For this to happen, learning systems have to be in place to generate, capture, and disseminate learnings across the enterprise. The I-mentor community functions as one means of storing and reusing knowledge. Another, more scaleable method is to use a knowledge management system, but one that has a human touch.

The Role of Knowledge Management

Knowledge management has gotten a bad rap. Many companies build knowledge management systems that become money pits or quickly become obsolete. When we started innovation at Whirlpool, we built a knowledge management system. The warnings were everywhere—they don't work; they get so big that no one uses them; they are hard to keep current; they often die of their own weight. Unfortunately, some of those warnings come true for Whirlpool.

In the first several years, we built the knowledge management system that we described in *Strategic Innovation* (Snyder and Duarte, 2003). Over the years, however, the utility of the knowledge management system has changed. It started out simply as an additional way to connect without face-to-face interaction. In the succeeding years, the I-pipe portion of knowledge management served as both a means of sharing knowledge and a measuring tool that became hardwired to the financials of the company. Every few years, we refresh the knowledge management system to ensure that it keeps up with embedded innovation. Even with our effort to keep it on track, the system becomes dormant and stale, so we have to strategize about what to do next. Recall that the Centralpark team did not go to the knowledge management system to find similar innovations. Although our system is impressive, it is still not driving the results that we had hoped for. The effort to hardwire it to the businesses and make it mainstream is a continuing struggle.

Although our knowledge management system has had its ups and downs and continues to present challenges, we continue to work on it. Why? Managing knowledge by organizing it, making it available, and improving it as one learns is a function critical to embedded innovation. In innovation from everyone and everywhere, knowledge needs to be open and democratized. In embedded innovation, knowledge management offers benefits to people who value learning. The first benefit is that innovators have access to knowledge that before sat at the top of silos or was available only to a few experts. Learning more about the company and the company's knowledge assets is not trivial. The second benefit is a social or network learning that groups of innovators share and pass on to succeeding groups of innovators. In essence, this social network learning becomes embedded and stimulates the creation of an innovation culture.

The Passion for Learning

Learning is one of the emotional drivers that attract people to innovation. Although other initiatives have learning opportunities, the opportunities to learn from embedded innovation are unique. They include learning about the world, the business, social networks, and oneself. The possibilities for learning are as varied as the innovators, and that is part of the attraction. Adult learners need control over their learning process. It must adapt to their unique needs.

As innovation becomes more and more embedded, we see the passion for learning grow. This passion is evident in each innovation team. In innovation, there is multidisciplinary learning within teams. In one case, the divergent thinkers on an innovation team conducted the tasks of thinking expansively and collecting insights, while the other team members who were not as motivated by learning took the role of converging the insights into a decision tree for the team to use to choose which insights to pursue. There is a place for everyone. Even the team members who may not be motivated by learning new information can be motivated by learning about new people in the social network of innovation. It is rare to find someone who is not motivated by at least one of the different types of learning that innovation offers.

In addition, a passion for learning can develop across the whole organization, especially if people see some immediate successes come out of the innovation work. The passion for learning creates an engaged and motivated group of innovators whose enthusiasm spills over into other aspects of their jobs. The motivation to gain new skills and information paired with the passion to learn creates a workforce that is more ready for change because they are creating it.

Embedded innovation entrenches innovation into a rational framework while also creating an environment that sanctions and reclaims our human need to learn, create, and dream. Learning is both a process and an outcome, and it occurs at the level of the individual, team, and organization. Learning associated with embedded innovation has unique traits and offers three types of learning: expansive thinking, idea forming, and problem solving. Imagine the power of an enterprise where everyone is finding the "aha" and WOW in learning that leads to bottom-line innovation results.

9

DREAM

Dreaming is an act of pure imagination, attesting in
all men a creative power, which if it were available
in waking, would make every man a Dante or
Shakespeare.

—*H. F. Hedge*

Great leaders in history knew the power of a dream. Mohandas
Gandhi, John F. Kennedy, and Martin Luther King Jr. all had
and shared great dreams that changed the world. But dreams
are not the domain solely of great world leaders. Dreams are
part of our everyday experience. Each of us has dreams that
empower us. Dreams big and small cause us to marshal our
resources in the attempt to fulfill them. They open us to new
experiences and create knowledge and passion. But if dreams are
part of daily existence and such a powerful source for change,
why have we stifled dreams in organizations?

Dreams are an unearthly and illusive concept. They present an unseen dimension that is both real and unreal at the
same time. For many people, dreaming has no place at work.
Dreaming is deeply rooted in our lives, yet many people do
not feel comfortable sharing their dreams, especially in a work
setting. This makes bringing dreams to the forefront a unique
characteristic of embedded innovation. There are few places in
organizations where the common person can dream, but innovation open to everyone is one of them.

This chapter shows that dreams are part of the human experience and that dreamers can find an outlet in innovation when
it is available to everyone. We explore the power of dreams,

show how dreams can solve very practical problems at work, and explain why organizations often resist dreams. Finally we show how three specific varieties of dreams can be used as part of the innovation process in a way that contributes to creating knowledge and becoming a learning organization.

The Power of Dreams

In the most practical sense, dreams are the skill to invent commercial realities from diverse knowledge of the world. Innovation offers dreams and dreamers a path to fulfilling hopes and passions. Dreams offer a source of ideas, a learning mechanism for innovators. Dreams also inspire hard work. One individual contributor from Whirlpool's engagement survey discussed how dreams turn into actions: "Nothing is as satisfying and engaging as when you set up dream goals, work hard with the right strategy and values to achieve them, enjoy the journey, and celebrate all small and big victories with the team. When a team member comes and thanks me saying 'you made a difference, hence I could give my best,' it makes me feel good, and I feel that I made my small contribution to my work. This becomes the reason for me to be more engaged happily and gives me energy. It starts with a dream." Embedded innovation, where everyone is innovating, offers a dream multiplier based on the number of people innovating every day.

Further, dreams accelerate growth that leads to learning for the innovator and for the organization. Dreams are part of thinking and the generation of knowledge from experience. Night dreams and daydreams are a way for people to learn through creating possibilities, reflection, and insights that may not be available to them in the waking hours.

Many people do their best problem solving in the shower. According to Boeddrich (2004), ideas emerge from the subconscious during activities that promote alpha waves in the brain, such as daydreaming, jogging, or taking a shower. It is also in this relaxed state that the conjunction of the problem with an item not related to it can help form a solution. We know conjunctions between two dissimilar entities are central to innovation and demonstrate the need to bring dreaming back into the workplace.

Whereas Freud saw dreams as insights into the *dreamer*, modern social scientists see dreams as ways to reveal thinking and feelings through insights into the *dream*. This shift to the dream itself becomes the practical shift that takes the mystery out of dreams and looks at them as insights or sources of information that will help create solutions. Most of the literature on applying dreams to waking life concerns a wide array of problems the dreamer wants to solve, related to such issues as relationships or health problems, but we want to look at dreams as they relate to commercial innovations.

The Idea Multiplier Effect of Dreams

Dreams create ideas. When different people bring their dreamed ideas together, those ideas feed off of each other and multiply. The following describes what we see as the logical flow for understanding how dreams contribute to innovation:

The more dreamers, the more dreams.

The more dreams, the more insights.

The more insights, the more intersections among them.

The more intersections, the greater the possibility for unique ideas.

The more unique ideas, the more innovations.

Therefore, the more dreamers there are, the greater the potential for innovations.

This logic also makes a compelling argument for embedded innovation from everyone as opposed to other types of innovation approaches that make innovation the province of a few. Of course, this logic will not work with an ineffective rational framework or if there are inadequate emotional drivers attracting innovators through free will. But with the proper rational framework and emotional drivers, more dreamers doing more dreaming will mean more ideas. Then the ideas are developed and refined—and weak ideas weeded out—in the innovation process. When an innovation process puts dreams to work, those dreams become ingredients for innovations.

Dreams at Work

When you dream at night, your mind is still working. As we just mentioned, it is in this subconscious state that often solutions arise that are unavailable to you during your waking hours. Dreamers can put their dreams to work; some researchers call these management dreams, where "management" refers to dreams that people use in their waking life.

Sims (2000) wrote an interesting dissertation on using dreams as solutions for management problems. She discusses how a management dream helps the dreamer solve work problems in a contextual framework. She proposes that strong needs (the struggle) trigger management dreams. One such contextual framework is the innovation process. Occasionally innovators can put their dreams to work or incubate them ahead of time to come up with a solution. They try to find solutions by willing themselves to dream about a perplexing problem.

Dreams can help in the learning phases of innovation, both in idea forming and problem solving. Dreamers can spend great amounts of time studying the problem in their waking hours, especially if they have an emotional connection to the problem. Recall from Chapter Two Pam Rogers's description of the early days of the Gladiator GarageWorks product line when the core team worked relentlessly to solve the problem. It is in this agitated state that dreams occasionally help solve the problem.

Of course, dreams are usually secondary sources of problem solving, but there are many examples in the innovation annals where dreams created a tipping point for the innovator.

One such innovator is Isaac Merrit Singer, the inventor of the sewing machine, who struggled with the needle mechanism of the machine. The orthodoxy Singer needed to overturn concerned the location of the hole in the needle used for sewing by hand; the hole was at the top of the needle. However, this would not work for a sewing machine. One night he had a dream about knights on horseback with their lances at their side. For some inexplicable reason, at the end of each lance was a hole. Because of this dream, Singer realized that the hole needed to be at the bottom tip of the needle, not at the top. Another famous dream put to work was the dream of Dmitri Ivanovich Mendeleev, the inventor of the periodic table of elements. The table structure came to him in a dream. In his waking hours he refined it and worked on it for over a decade, but the breakthrough was from a dream.

A more recent example comes to mind. I worked with Barbara Rand, a talented I-mentor we've mentioned elsewhere in this book, on LWE—Whirlpool's executive education initiative using innovation tools (described in Chapter Four). The team she was facilitating had come to an impasse by the end of the day, so they agreed to pick up the following day to work through their problem. When I saw Barbara the next morning, I innocently asked her as a greeting, "How did you sleep?" Barbara said she had slept poorly, and in the wee hours of the morning she had awakened with the impasse on her mind. She realized that she had been struggling with the team's problem in her sleep. At two she got up and designed a solution for the team. She tried it the next day, leading to a breakthrough.

Dupont teaches innovators how to capture and interpret dreams. They have applied this technique to innovate solutions to problems. Dupont teaches innovators to keep a pad and pencil by their bed to jot down their dreams and then to interpret the dreams' meaning in relation to the problems. One factory was having trouble with vacuum hoses collapsing. One night, one of the vendors dreamed of Slinky toys. After that, he applied a springlike mechanism to the hoses, which successfully prevented the hoses from collapsing. It took a dream to create the fuzzy front end to the problem resolution. One manager in the Whirlpool engagement survey said, "As a team we should get together at least twice a year for a think tank to bounce ideas off each other, inspire each other, and work through the difficult times that we all face. We should adopt this 'One Team One Dream' policy and have a buddy system with a member from another location, to constantly keep in contact with and come up with dreams to further grow the business."

Psychological researchers Schredl and Erlacher (2007) studied how people who recalled their dreams differ from those who don't. One category they looked at was dreams that stimulated people to think of doing something new in their waking life. They cited one study in which filmmakers, as a subset, reported that dreams affected their waking-life creative activities at a higher rate than did the general population of the study. In their study, Schredl and Erlacher found that the greatest number of applications of creative dreaming related to traditional jobs rather than to other applications, such as music or writing. In summary, they found that individuals with average levels of creativity, not creative geniuses, reported that dreams stimulated their waking life problem solving.

When we dream, we are thinking. The hectic workday most of us experience leaves us with little time to "think." Innovation, especially the first stages in ideation, causes people to think and allows innovators the space for the freedom to think. Perhaps it is this space to dream that creates innovation, more than the process, tools, or even the rational framework.

Resistance to Dreams at Work

Although dreams can be powerful, they are often resisted in organizations. One reason is that dreams are often a metaphor for possibilities. Thinking about possibilities is a risky proposition in most companies because the organizational culture does not encourage people to think about what *could be*. Instead, organizations tend to reinforce the status quo or the incremental improvement of *what is*. Allowing people to talk about dreams gives the dreamer permission to try out-of-the-box thinking, to "clean sheet" it. Possibilities are usually positive views of the future that teams use to get over the idea struggle. Innovation helps innovators create possibilities from new information and ideation sessions. Many people are natural "possibility thinkers" and find a safe and satisfying home in innovation.

Another reason dreams are resisted at work is that many people, even people who recall dreams, do not trust dreams for solving problems, even as a secondary set of insights. They do not trust their own dreams as a source for learning. Secretan (2006) writes that while we have expanded our ability to quantify and measure, we have stifled our ability to dream. We don't use dreams or talk about dreams in companies. We couch dreams in mission statements or visions. He contends that dreams transcend differences as nothing else can; they create oneness. (This concerns the last emotional driver, the spirit of winning from embedded innovation, which we will discuss in Chapter Twelve.)

Embedded innovation requires dreaming at work; dreams become a form of thinking to create new knowledge. Once they are demystified, they can be used as one of the many sources of insight. We have seen innovators—even left-brained, rational, no-nonsense quantoids—become so passionate about their problem that they do not discriminate against dreams as sources of ideas.

Unleashing dreams at work requires giving people the freedom to challenge conventional wisdom and the status quo. When we dream of possibilities, we are imagining an alternative future. Imagination is the ability to invent alternatives from known knowledge and perceptions of the world. Imagination is a key part of the innovation process, but there are conditions required to unleash it. There needs to be a freedom to think, take risks, and try new things. There also has to be a freedom to overcome the idea struggle and a rule not to judge innovators prematurely as they envision a future.

Do the people at your company have the freedom to dream?

Varieties of Dreams

The word *dream* has multiple meanings. First, there is the act of having a dream, either asleep at night or in a daydream. In either case, a team ideation process where dreams merge with other dreams to create *social dreams* can help bring ideas from the subconscious into the workplace. The second way to think about the term dream is as the vision or imagination to think outside the box—dreaming up a vision or future, such as Martin Luther King's vision of racial equality. At Whirlpool we call this the *dreamspace*. The final way we look at dreams is in terms of the dreamer's own hopes or personal aspirations. These are dreams about what we want to accomplish personally. Innovation creates a beacon for people who desire fulfillment of these three types of dreams.

Dreams and problem solving can help in other initiatives, such as cost reduction or total quality management, but dreaming in innovation has a payoff that nothing else in corporate life can give. Dreams lead people to innovation, and when innovation is open to all, it draws in dreamers who sometimes have no other outlet for their dreams.

Social Dreams

Social dreaming is the web of thinking and passion that underpins the social networks that create innovations. In innovation, social dreaming—or what Lawrence (2003) refers to as the social dream matrix—legitimizes dreaming by bringing it into a team format to generate ideas as people meet together and share their dreams. The power of social dreaming first comes from the interactions between dreams and then the successive ideas that follow from the interactions, the set of secondary ideas. As innovation teams keep adding new knowledge and new dreams to their domain, more and more possibilities arise. Creating ideas in a social dream network is not only productive but also fun and exciting. We believe it is this process, which at Whirlpool we call *ideation*, that enrolls people to innovation. We want to use the term *social dreaming* here to get *inside* ideation and describe what occurs to form new or unique ideas.

The social dream matrix is not an embedded innovation "tool" in itself, but a concept that describes how innovation teams create new knowledge that is essential to innovation. The interactions of a dream matrix can lead to innovations at any point in the I-pipe. One illustration of a social dream matrix is the interactions that innovators create in computer-aided idea generation. Here the social matrix is a virtual format where ideas and dreams intersect over the Internet to form new knowledge. The quintessential social dream matrix occurs when in a team interaction one member tells the group about his or her dream. As a result, another team member says, "While you were talking, it made me think about X." That exact intersection is where innovators can create new knowledge. The social dream matrix helps overcome the idea struggle to get the best ideas from people's heads into the innovation process.

There is safety in the social dream matrix of innovation. The team aspect of sharing ideas or dreams grants permission to bring dreams to the forefront and try them out in light of other dreams. "I have made bigger dreams look simpler by having everyone in the team contribute and share [in the dream]," one person wrote in a Whirlpool engagement survey. When the social dreaming matrix is part of an innovation process, new organization capability forms. The social dream matrix opens spaces for thinking and sharing that are safe for everyone who engages in innovation. The variety of dreams and thinking exponentially increases the number of new ideas that can be fodder for innovations. The organizational tools and processes of embedded innovation sanction dreaming and thinking as a source of knowledge.

Social dreaming promotes learning. It is a basic premise that the mind grows from exploring the unknown. Some innovators call this kind of exploration the negative capacity; exploring the known is positive capacity. Negative capacity allows an innovation team to work at the edge of the unknown and look for patterns through dreaming and thinking that lead to new knowledge or ideas, creating a practical tension between the known and the unknown. As Lawrence (2003) states, dreams access the infinite. The new knowledge created through social dreaming engenders great passion and excitement. Innovators thrive on creating knowledge that can lead to unique solutions. Another benefit is that social dreaming often unleashes hidden or unspoken knowledge about an organization or its products and services. Social dreaming can create mini revolutions to overthrow orthodoxies and can mobilize teams into action to find solutions.

Dreamspace

A second type of dream leads to a vision or a future reality. The work of strategic planning often starts with the formation of a vision. Strategic planning legitimizes dreaming and renames it—*vision, end state*, or *outcome*—to make it palatable in the business world. In innovation, dreams have a specific purpose: they generate a vision of the innovation. In embedded innovation, we call the vision a dreamspace.

Asking innovators to create a dreamspace makes dreaming part of the process. People are drawn to innovation because they want to create and fulfill dreams about solutions or themselves. A dreamspace is what Collins and Porras (1996) call the envisioned future, both a big hairy audacious goal and a vivid description of the future. The vivid description forces the strategist to think of the vision as a story to share so as to motivate people toward the envisioned future. At Whirlpool, we use two innovation tools from the Strategos' toolkit, migration paths and dreamspaces, to help innovators envision the biggest business possible from their ideas.

Dreamspaces force innovation teams to describe blue oceans. A dreamspace is a way to articulate a vision for an innovation opportunity and to organize the ideas into logical groupings called migration paths. The paths are parallel plans to reach the dreamspace. In a sense, the migration path plots a collection of ideas that lead to the vision of the innovation. Figure 9.1 shows an example of a dreamspace for a search engine for researchers with unusual research needs. It also shows the "bones" of the migration path. Innovators take their

Figure 9.1 Dreamspace Example

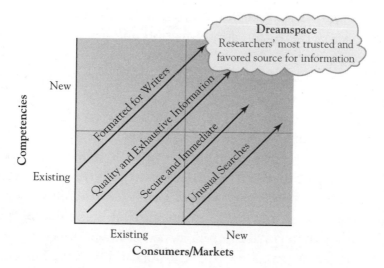

Source: Strategos, Inc. Used with permission.

ideas and post them on the migration path into groupings or bones. Innovators also iterate the dreamspace as they work on and refine their ideas.

Dreams as Personal Aspirations

A third kind of dream is an aspiration for the dreamer. Dreaming here involves imagining a future self, trying something different, being something else, and moving away from a routine and uninteresting job toward the excitement of innovation. In embedded innovation at Whirlpool, the dream can also be to change one's career to become an I-mentor.

Innovation opens new avenues for unbounded self-growth. It offers a chance for everyone to demonstrate his or her skills or intellect in a way that traditional jobs may not foster. It is also, to a few, a dream of being part of a team that creates the next set of Gladiator GarageWorks products. This is a hero's dream of invention. The hero's dream is similar to a dream of winning the lottery: the odds are small, but the dreamer nonetheless believes it is possible, and winning means fulfilling one's dreams. Writing in the journal *Creativity and Innovation Management*, Getz and Robinson (2003) describe the innovation jackpot as creating an innovation and getting rich on the needs and wants undreamed by anyone else. It is what attracts people to casinos or lotteries—the dream that a big bet will bring glory.

Embedded innovation is encompassing enough to create an environment that supports fulfillment of the variety of individual dreams. It offers dreamers the tools and framework to take control of fulfilling their dreams. It also offers an avenue to dream for the common good of the enterprise, move beyond one's job or silo, and work on meaningful and fulfilling projects. More than anything, embedded innovation grants control to dreamers to follow their passion and dreams. Embedded innovation that includes everyone in the possibilities weaves a safety net to allow people to go beyond personal or professional limitations.

Connections with Other Emotional Drivers

Dreaming has unique connections to the other emotional drivers, as illustrated in Figure 9.2. It connects to heroes by creating innovation folklore about people who use dreams to change the world. Dreaming connects to learning because dreams are a secondary source of insight and are accelerators of learning. Dreams create an esprit de corps through social or organization dreams, and dreams are a key ingredient to creativity.

Figure 9.2 Intersections of Emotional Drivers of Embedded Innovation: Dream

Dream	Create	Heroes	Spirit
• Accelerating learning through dreams • Learning to use dreams	• Creating new knowledge • Learning valuable and fun tools	• Fulfilling a journey of self-discovery • Forming ideas and problem solving	• Creating a learning organization
	• Dreaming of possibilities	• Fulfilling dream of new identity • Following dreams to self-fulfillment	• Creating esprit de corps through group dreams
		• Unlocking creativity • Creating more heroes	• Engaging and attracting potential innovators
			• Revitalizing the organization • Creating mythology and cultural norms

Learn →
Dream →
Create →
Heroes →

Imagine a company of dreamers. Imagine hundreds, thousands, or tens of thousands of people so emotionally attached to possibilities that they put their dreams to work to realize them. With the help of the rational framework and the emotional drivers of creating, learning, heroes, and a spirit of innovation, dreamers can innovate and create differentiated products, services, and day-to-day work processes that impact the bottom line and unleash human potential.

10

CREATE

Whatever creativity is, it is in part a solution to
a problem.

—*Brian Aldiss*

When we started our efforts to embed innovation at Whirlpool, we did not spend time or money trying to make people more creative. A key principle underlying embedded innovation is that people are inherently creative and have the desire, skills, and need to create and innovate. This chapter covers the evidence and reasoning underlying this principle and some of the ways we unleashed the inherent need to create across the organization by removing the structural barriers to creativity. It also covers some of the unexpected benefits of these activities.

For the purposes of embedded innovation, we define creativity as "the ability to solve problems that are worth solving. It is the ability to create knowledge" (Taking Children Seriously, 2008). Creativity is necessary but not sufficient for innovation. For an idea, service, or product to be innovative, it must also be considered useful and result in some sort of permanent change in society or the way we live, think, and work. Our experience at Whirlpool suggests that just as people are inherently creative, they also have a need to have those ideas translate into something that is valued and useful to others.

Creating is the action that turns dreams into reality. Creating is the way that people engage in the innovation process and put into action what they dream about and have learned. Creating can take many forms: new products, services, features, buying experiences, or ways to serve

Whirlpool's customers, trade partners, the local community, and the larger world.

Our job at Whirlpool is to structure an environment where this human need to create can be fulfilled at work. Most organizations, especially ones that are older and more established, have built-in structural mechanisms that actually block creativity. We needed to address these barriers and free our people to create. We also had to provide the rational architecture and tools for people to translate their creativity into value for the corporation. The goal is to allow people to create and then translate that creativity into innovations that align with corporate objectives and create competitive advantage. Figure 10.1 shows how creating connects with the other emotional drivers.

Figure 10.1 Intersections of Emotional Drivers of Embedded Innovation: Create

Dream	Create	Heroes	Spirit
• Accelerating learning through dreams • Learning to use dreams **(Learn →)**	• Creating new knowledge • Learning valuable and fun tools	• Fulfilling a journey of self-discovery • Forming ideas and problem solving	• Creating a learning organization
(Dream →)	• Dreaming of possibilities	• Fulfilling dream of new identity • Following dreams to self-fulfillment	• Creating esprit de corps through group dreams
	(Create →)	• Unlocking creativity • Creating more heroes	• Engaging and attracting potential innovators
		(Heroes →)	• Revitalizing the organization • Creating mythology and cultural norms

Cultural Barriers to Creativity

When we first began to embed innovation at Whirlpool, we were fully aware that our environment had, over the years, become very process oriented and somewhat bureaucratic. Although there were clear pockets of innovation and creativity and a few products that could be described as innovations, Whirlpool's leaders realized that we were not as innovative as we needed to be to remain competitive. In the decade before we started embedded innovation, Whirlpool had tried creativity training, outsourcing creativity to outside companies around new products and services, and other tactics. None of these efforts were sustainable. Although the creativity classes were fun, the lessons learned were rarely transferred back into the organization. As with many training classes, the skills, tools, and applicability faded once people got back on the job.

Even before we started embedded innovation, we started to take a different tack: instead of framing the issue as a people problem (that our people didn't know how to be creative), we asked if it was an organizational problem. Were we blocking creativity? As a result of this shift in approach, for three years running, the senior management team surveyed members of the workforce to determine the barriers to creativity and innovation. During those three years, we took different approaches to answering the question, How can we allow the workforce to be more creative and innovative? We sent out paper surveys, interviewed people, and used Web-based methods. The answers always came back the same. A few of the key findings over these three years are presented here. (You might recognize your own company.)

Anyone can say "no." Many people believed that when someone did have a creative idea, almost anyone above or beside that person could say no to it. They said that it was just too hard to buck everyone's opinions and experience, and many gave up trying after a few times. Interviewees described the idea evaluation process as having too many layers of scrutiny before ideas could make it to where they could have a true test in the marketplace.

The company is overly process oriented and internally focused. Many people believed that one of Whirlpool's biggest strengths was its process orientation, in terms of operational excellence, ISO 9000, Baldrige, product development, and other areas. Many thought, however, that an unintended consequence of this strength was that it also stifled creativity. In other words, the processes were good for repeatable events, but created an orientation to work that was mechanical and internally focused.

The company had grown risk averse. Most respondents stated that over the years Whirlpool had become highly risk averse and followed a "me too" strategy.

There is a lack of incentive to be creative. People told us that the goal-setting, performance management, and compensation systems did not support, recognize, or reward creativity. Many also reported that their jobs did not have a creative component that was formally recognized. This is probably related to the process orientation that had developed over a number of years.

There is no structure or forum for creativity. Finally, many people felt that the company lacked a structure, forum, or set of people to foster creativity. People with a creative idea didn't know whom to take it to or what to do with it. We also received comments about the stovepiped nature of the organization and the lack of interaction between functions and regions around new product development, management practices, and problem solving.

Some of the descriptions of the environment for innovation in Whirlpool are instructive:

> "Lots of creative people and ideas but an environment that does not nurture this."
>
> "Ready, aim, aim, aim, aim . . ."

In other words, we did not as an organization support creativity; we favored analysis over action; people felt frozen; and we had no follow-through when people presented interesting ideas.

Developing a Receptive Culture for Creativity

As a result of these findings and still before embedded innovation, we came to understand that the problem with creativity was not the people and their skills, but the culture and set of management and leadership practices and processes that had developed over the years. Our greatest strength, as typically happens, had also become our greatest weakness: a focus on process, repeatability, and predictability. We knew we needed to address leader behavior, processes, and culture to unleash the creativity inherent in our people.

We had just come off of another "culture" effort focused on values and inclusion in the workplace. These are of course related to creativity in terms of valuing everyone's ideas, but how many culture efforts could we have? Wisely, the management team decided not to initiate another culture effort, but instead to assume that our people were inherently creative. (We offer some insights on cultural change in the Conclusion.) The team decided to address the topics outlined in the previous section through embedded innovation instead of a cultural change initiative per se to facilitate creativity and to remove barriers. A major part of our effort, of course, was to reengineer our processes to align with the strategic architecture for innovation, as we described in Part Two. As part of this process, we focused on the areas we discuss in the following sections. These are steps any company can take to develop an environment that fulfills the inherent need for all of us to create, and to ensure that creativity is transferred to business results.

Balance Process Orientation with Flexibility

For a process-oriented company like Whirlpool, adding the ability to be flexible can be vexing. We found that you need to be careful not to upset the advantages of processes that are valuable and certainly not to show disrespect for the time and effort many individuals have put into creating processes and systems that, in many cases, provide competitive advantage. At Whirlpool, we decided to create a set of "criteria" for how processes should align to the new goals of innovation and have each process owner review his or her processes for alignment with the new vision around innovation. We asked these process owners to focus on such criteria as how they provide incentives, encourage creative thinking, enable alignment with consumer insights, maximize ideation, and create room for management process innovation.

You can ask process owners at your company to examine their processes in light of criteria you develop for innovation and in light of the company's vision for innovation, to ensure that their processes maintain a good balance between retaining the competitive advantages that your processes promote and making room for creativity and aligning with the goals of innovation.

No processes should be exempt from this request. Processes examined should include product development, performance management, rewards and bonuses, education and leadership development, operational excellence, and customer care, among others.

Give Creativity a Time, Place, and Structure

At Whirlpool, the rational drivers are designed to provide a time, place, and structure for creativity. A critical component to the rational drivers is the I-mentor program. As we have mentioned in other parts of this book, becoming an I-mentor means taking time away from the duties associated with everyday roles. The I-pipe also enables creativity and channels it toward meaningful business results.

If your company wants to make innovation from everyone and everywhere a reality, you must be flexible enough to give people time to innovate. At the beginning of the S-curve, the question is, Can people get away from their everyday jobs to explore new possibilities? As you move up the S-curve, the question should be, Is it part of people's job to take the time to explore new possibilities? You also need to provide structures and support for people with ideas; this includes training and an I-pipe process that people can use to develop their ideas.

The vision of innovation from everyone, everywhere allowed Whirlpool and its people to create the time and space for creativity. It also offered a way for Whirlpool to work at being creative into everyone's job.

Provide Tools That Enable Creativity

Although people have an inherent need and ability to be creative, training and tools can help them be even more creative and, more important, establish a common language and process to help teams create. A fundamental premise of almost all the tools used in the ideation stage of the innovation process is that we need to broaden our thinking based on customer insights, external trends, and other sources of information before we evaluate ideas. The tools that we started with are Strategos' intellectual property and will not be reproduced in this book. However, with Strategos' permission, we look deeper at two examples to illustrate how tools can help innovation teams be creative. Strategos' tools are outstanding.

The following are two of the techniques that were most effective in the "expansive thinking" phase:

Orthodoxies exercise. This exercise promotes creative thinking by allowing creators to examine unspoken assumptions and how those assumptions might be affecting their ability to be creative. The exercise involves a group brainstorming session that presents the question, "What would customer X, Y, or Z *never* say about us?" This is a fun way to expose the orthodoxies we carry around about any situation, product, or service. Once these are uncovered and examined, they can be creatively explored with the question, "What if we were to overturn these orthodoxies?" We've already mentioned the overturning of the "all Whirlpool customers are women" orthodoxy that led to Gladiator GarageWorks. Another orthodoxy exposed in this exercise was that there is only one economic engine in our industry. When we challenged that assumption and imagined there being more than one—a subscription model, for example—we were on our way to creating EcoHouse, the trusted water service innovated by Whirlpool Brazil, which is showing promising results.

Lens smashing. This is another creativity technique that broadens innovators' thinking. In lens smashing, as we described in Chapter Five, dissimilar ideas are "smashed" together to get creative ideas flowing. Whirlpool used this method and began to smash together trends, customer benefits, overturned orthodoxies, and new economic engines to look for creative ideas. For example, one lens might be a working mother's perspective of a product, feature, service, or the purchase experience; we could smash that lens with that of customization to come up with a feature that allows people who are busy to customize their purchase experience based on their needs and schedule.

These represent just two of the examples of creative thinking techniques. But creativity techniques themselves are not really the most important part of the message. They are common and can come from many sources. What is important is to provide a safe environment to use these techniques during training and to encourage their use when people go back to their daily job. Methods to think more expansively will start showing up in many places: during offsite retreats to consider new ways of doing business, in training focused on customer-centered operational excellence, in thinking about how staff organizations could be more customer focused, in community service, and more.

Help People Say Yes

Any organization that has been around awhile accumulates people who have worked in a number of different functions in the organization over a long period and have become "experts" not only in their technical discipline but in the organization and its history. These individuals remember everything that was ever tried, successfully and otherwise. They are the keepers of the company's history, and as such, they feel that it is their job, and duty, to protect the company from newcomers or those with crazy ideas. Because they understand the nuances of the organization, they can protect it from ideas that have failed before.

Whirlpool decided that these experienced managers were valuable assets to the organization. Instead of trying to change them, we created several structures that incentivized people to listen to and try out new ideas. The first was the mandatory use of "seed funds" for new ideas. When Whirlpool first started our innovation effort, Dave Whitwam made the handing out of seed funds for new ideas mandatory. He wanted to move resources close to the ideas. Each region had a fund; he also set up his own seed fund and got the word out that if the region turned you down, you could come to him and he would fund your idea. This mandate sent a strong message that new ideas are important and to be nurtured. Of course, creative ideas that used the innovation process would be funded. Interestingly, Whitwam never had to dip into his seed fund; the businesses used their seed money to fund many ideas.

The second way to make it everyone's job to say yes was to establish the I-boards. Through these boards, leaders could become part of a process that looked at creative ideas with the task of ensuring that some of them made it into experimentation. The actual role of these leaders was to select creative ideas that would create competitive advantage.

Another way that Whirlpool made it everyone's job to foster creativity was to change the performance management system such that leaders' degree of involvement in innovation efforts throughout the year became part of their appraisal. The appraisal also assessed the degree to which they had encouraged their employees to take part in innovation teams and in I-mentor training. Thus leaders were actually assessed on how well they supported innovation efforts.

If you want to encourage innovation at your company, you need to help leaders at all levels say yes. Although saying "We tried that once, and it didn't work" can sometimes provide valuable information, it often just stops the flow of ideas. Managers who rush to judgment need to be encouraged to talk less and listen more. Whirlpool set up budgets, structures, and performance management systems to provide incentives for listening and trying new ideas. What can you do at your company?

Manage Risk Taking

To live in an innovative space requires an appropriate orientation to risk. Whirlpool had to match how it addressed risk with its new goal of embedding innovation from everyone everywhere. Clearly no one wants to go to market with products that don't make money, but there needs to be a way to test creative ideas for new products and services and simultaneously to manage risk. The approach that we take is to create a set of managed experiments in the market with new products and services. Instead of managing risk by eliminating any new idea, by saying no, or by just adopting ideas after your competitors do, consider designing a set of progressive experiments in the market with target customers, and using the results to hone and focus creative ideas. This way, people can feel free to be creative in the expansive part of the innovation process, knowing that the market and customers will shape the ideas to be competitive when the time is right. This approach has worked well at Whirlpool.

Have Patience

Wild ideas for the sake of wild ideas are not what creativity is about. Creative ideas, at some point, need to be aligned with customer insights and be a viable way to make money in the market.

With that said, you also need to have patience while the people in the organization and the management of the company learn how to be creative. There will be false starts, and ideas that could not possibly make it in the marketplace will sometimes get too far along the I-pipe. For example, one innovation team came up with an idea for a bicycle with a computer display on it. This was in 2000, long before the current Internet connectivity craze. Another team came up with an unattended safe box outside one's home for deliveries; it was on a migration path to be refrigerated or heated for food deliveries. Giving innovators a sandbox that is broad enough to capture their imagination and motivate creatively is one of the best ways to create a culture of yes.

Today Whirlpool has brought creativity in line with customer focus and strategic direction. But it took a great deal of patience. Don't expect to move up the S-curve rapidly. There is no creativity without trial and error.

Diversity and Creativity

Our efforts to unleash people's natural creativity at Whirlpool have paid a big, unexpected return. Whirlpool, like many other organizations, is concerned with ensuring diversity in its workplace and ensuring that everyone's perspective, background, and point of view are included and valued. Whirlpool has focused on ensuring this diversity in a number of different ways, from a corporate value that focuses on diversity, to diversity councils and groups, to training and education on diversity and inclusion.

The reasons for this focus on diversity, beyond the fact that it is simply the right thing to do, are at least threefold:

1. Demographics and societies are changing, not only in the United States but around the world. If Whirlpool's demographics mirror those of society in general, people inside the company should be better able to understand customer insights and thus ensure that Whirlpool's products and services are keeping up with demographic changes.

2. Good talent is scarce, and to attract the best and the brightest, Whirlpool needs to ensure that it can pull talent from everyone, everywhere. The diversity of the workforce is one indicator that many individuals look at to decide if a company matches their lifestyle.

3. All research on creativity shows that diverse perspectives lead to more creative ideas.

Before we began to embed innovation, our diversity efforts certainly raised awareness, but they did not achieve the results we needed; such metrics as the types of diverse thinking that lead to new ideas or the level of diversity on teams and in senior positions were still not where Whirlpool wanted them to be.

Then came our innovation effort. It had an interesting and unexpected impact. Because the most creative ideas were getting play and being funded for experiments, groups began to seek diversity, as it became increasingly apparent that the most diverse groups and innovation teams had the most creative ideas that translated customer insights into new products and services. Without any explicit work or focus on diversity, the innovation effort became a driving force in supporting, promoting, and enabling diversity. There is no better business case for diversity than innovation.

Creating an Environment That Fosters Creativity

One of our fundamental assumptions is that people are inherently creative and have a need to create. As we've noted throughout this book, it is the work environment that often prevents the expression of these natural drives. Table 10.1 is a checklist to see if your environment is conducive to creativity.

Table 10.1 Environmental Assessment for Embedded Innovation

Activity	Yes	No
Our performance management system has specific goals and metrics related to fostering creativity.	☐	☐
Leaders and managers are expected to listen to and "fund" creative ideas, in the arena of management processes as well as products and services.	☐	☐
There is a way for people with creative ideas to get seed money, time, or other resources to try out new ideas.	☐	☐
There is a formal method to manage risk associated with putting new ideas into practice, either in the marketplace or internally through experimentation in management processes.	☐	☐
We have examined our systems and processes to see if they are stifling creativity and have adjusted them accordingly.	☐	☐
People are provided with a structure and time and space to be creative—it is part of the job, not an adjunct accountability.	☐	☐
We allow trial and error and have patience in expecting results from creativity.	☐	☐
Our leadership team holds the fundamental assumption that people are inherently creative and that we need to help them in the quest to fulfill this need.	☐	☐

To create is a basic human desire that has been stifled by over one hundred years of management theory that removes creativity from the workplace. Embedded innovation creates an environment that not only allows creativity but requires it. Unleashing creativity starts with building the machine that makes innovation possible and then helping innovators with tools and processes for turning their creativity into innovations. If you can accomplish this, the creativity in your people will surface. Embedded innovation creates a space for creativity not only to flourish but to have real business impact.

11

HEROES

Heroes create circumstances; circumstances
create heroes.

—*Chinese proverb*

Heroes inspire us. We want to emulate them. We want to share in
their acclaim. If you could, you would create hundreds, thousands
of innovation heroes. But you do not "create" innovation heroes
(I-heroes). There is no spell to conjure or magic potion you can
use. They are a gift from the innovation gods. The best you can do
is to create the environment and rational framework that enables
innovation and allow the heroes to find you.

Whereas the emotional drivers of learning, dreaming, and
creating are all actions and are essential in order to innovate,
heroes refers to the people (both individuals and teams) who
innovate; they are necessary to *sustain* embedded innovation over
time. Innovation always provokes resistance—even at Whirlpool.
Without heroes to lift our spirits, innovation can wither over
time. But with heroes to excite and sustain us, innovation from
everyone and everywhere becomes more than the fad of the
month or fad of the year—more than even a "major corporate initiative in the first decade of the twenty-first century"—it becomes
woven into the fabric of the company and its culture. If innovation heroes do not emerge of their own accord at your company,
then innovation is probably not embedded very deeply.

To gauge how well innovation is embedded in a company, you
need to go beyond measuring the results that come out of the I-
pipe. You also need to measure the success of embedded innovation by the heroic mythology it inspires and the magnitude and

frequency of stories that people share. Embedded innovation presents the possibility for anyone to become an innovator and possibly an I-hero. Companies can invest millions in a communication plan for innovation, but one successful shot heard 'round the world—a story of a team of "everyday" heroes—reverberates more quickly than the best communications deployment. Innovation creates stories of heroes, garage innovators, and teams of men and women who beat the odds by creating something new for the world. Innovation folklore passes from one group to the next. There is an innovation mythos about creating new products, services, or businesses. The hero can be an individual, a team, or a company. Take Spencer Silver. He became an I-hero as an inventor of glue that was not sticky enough. His name is not well known, but this I-hero of 3M accidentally discovered the glue used for Post-it notes. This is an example of innovation myth based in truth that we have all heard and retold to others. Innovation breeds stories about what the hero must endure to beat the odds, oftentimes through curious accidents or overturned orthodoxies.

How People Become Innovation Heroes

We use the term *hero* to apply to both men and women. A classical hero is someone who musters the courage to fulfill an achievement of higher purpose, usually with personal sacrifice. Heroes are not individual achievers who are only out for themselves. Although they may achieve a personal gain, such as overcoming a shortcoming, they must go through great personal risk and sacrifice for the good of their community or society, or for humankind. They are warriors who beat the odds and overcome obstacles to bring new knowledge or gifts to the world. Heroes go on a journey of change, personal growth.

Why are people perceived to be heroes? What confers hero status? People don't become heroes because management decides to hand out plaques at an award show.

I-heroes are perceived as genuine and are liked by their community. They are not self-glorifying. If innovators who succeed are not trusted or respected, they still can create remarkable innovations, but they will not be bestowed the respect of an I-hero. A person becomes an I-hero by an informal vote of the people. Whirlpool had a prolific innovator who was never revered as an I-hero. He was almost singularly responsible for some remarkable commercial innovation successes. However, when we asked people at Whirlpool whom they thought of as I-heroes, they did not mention him. When we asked about him, they were quick to discredit him and then went on to talk about someone they held in high esteem. I-heroes are not created, and their acclaim is hard to predict; their status is elusive. They are measured only by the respect and admiration of their peers within a company. I-hero status can only exist informally; to formalize it by making the identification and labeling of heroes a corporate initiative is to kill it. I-heroes are creations of the innovation mythology.

The reasons why people are perceived by their peers as I-heroes vary. An I-hero can be the person who comes up with the one great idea that moves the team forward or the person who is deeply committed to the innovation. I-heroes contribute big and small innovations. It is not just about creating a big, breakthrough innovation, although that helps. You don't have to invent the next iPod to be an I-hero. It is more about the dedication to your dream and beating the odds, standing up to the monsters of the status quo and "the way we always have done it."

To help understand this, we informally asked people who their Whirlpool I-heroes were and why they revere them. We wanted to learn the reasons one is granted the status of I-hero, so we conducted a survey to ask about these mythical creatures. We decided that it was more informative to look at the reasons behind selection of the I-heroes at Whirlpool than it was to look at the individuals themselves.

One person praised a team of I-heroes for their personal energy to drive their innovations. Another account was of the I-heroes who stayed with the idea long after it was "forgotten" and for working without acclaim through the grueling months to get it to market. One person spoke of a senior manager in Italy for his food preservation innovation and the belief that he was "risking his career" to pursue it. Another individual was anointed who partnered with Ferrari and other famous designer labels to market a clothes refresher in Europe. One team was lauded because of the personal beliefs they had about their product that were often at odds with the beliefs of the senior leaders. One woman in Italy was acclaimed as a serial innovator because she was the "driving force" behind many innovations. That force drove the "green kitchen," an innovation strategy creating a set of products to create a kitchen "ecosystem."

One person was distinguished because he drove the use of the innovation tools in productivity and cost improvements. Because of his innovation, there is the possibility now to identify more projects, with a potential of a $50 million cost reduction. One I-hero was revered because he chose to be a sponsor of innovation when it was not his job and when doing so might have been unpopular. One person was renowned because he is "everywhere" on the innovation landscape, reading, talking at conferences, and learning what there is to know about innovation. Core to the I-heroes of Whirlpool are personal risk, humility, being a team player, being a driving force, and following their passion.

In embedded innovation, there are fewer individual I-heroes than team I-heroes. As one of our Whirlpool colleagues in Brazil wrote, "As you know, Innovation has had many facets over these years and today the environment for Innovation is on product and in the region the process occurs during the fuzzy, front-end process for each product category. Instead of a one-person initiative, it is a collective process involving different people and areas who apply the innovation process."

The Hero's Journey

Joseph Campbell studied heroes in all cultures throughout recorded history. He traced the journeys of heroes and found that they all share common themes and traits. Campbell gained fame for his 1988 PBS series, *The Power of Myth,* with Bill Moyers. According to Campbell, the hero's journey consists of a calling, resisting and then accepting the call, overcoming barriers, and a great learning; in the end, the hero solves a problem for his or her group or community or for humankind.

The role of the hero in mythology is universal. At the heart of the hero's journey is a conflict between the hero's self-interest and the need to be part of a shared community. To resolve this conflict, the hero must follow her passion or the wisdom of her heart (Campbell, 1969).

Heroes and Myths

Mythology, according to Campbell, consists of stories about heroes that connect the audience of the story to their own lives within the context of a community or environment. Mythology is critical to culture. Campbell also believed that myths help shape individuals to their culture as they revitalize the world. He wrote that myths are as important in the present as they were in previous generations. Today, the learnings of heroes include change, personal learning, risk taking, and concern for the common good.

A mythology is a set of stories (myths), usually associated with a group, event, or institution. Myths are not always about gods or monsters. Often they are about a common person who answers a call for greatness. The mythology of heroes usually represents a set of beliefs and explains a practice, a rite of passage, or some aspect of life. We often think of myths as something invented or untrue, but myths are also stories based on truth and then stretched to make the legend memorable. Heroes, mythology, and myths have existed in every era and in every generation. Although most of us think of Greek gods when we think of mythology, much of our present-day mythology comprises sports, war heroes, everyday life, and work heroes. Many great movies or books use a mythical hero for the story. We tell or listen to the hero's story because there is an element of the hero that we recognize in ourselves. We learn from heroes because they somehow relate to our life. Deep inside, many people believe that they have the character to become a hero.

The I-Hero's Journey

It is true that not every innovator reaches hero status—as we discussed earlier, the status of hero is conferred by a person's peers based on personal risk, humility, being a team player, being a driving force, and following his passion. But many people do dream of recognition for their innovation efforts, whether or not they expect to become I-heroes. Many of us are motivated to stand out in a company, not for the sake of rank but because we want to become part of innovation legend. It is a paradox within us—humbly wanting to succeed solely for reasons of accomplishment, but also wanting recognition. The need for acclaim may not be the primary driver for innovators, but it is often a secondary one. If you ask innovators why they went through the pain and trials of innovating, they do not say that they wanted to be a hero or to be famous. Like gamblers who won't say aloud that they are trying to win big, so as not to tempt fate, we have an inner subtext that is saying, *I hope I win big.* And why not? It is how we are wired, to better ourselves and the world around us.

Schulman (1996) defines an organization hero as one who acts for a larger purpose in the face of risk and beyond the actions expected in the role he or she occupies. Using this definition as the basis, I-heroes are people who take actions to *innovate for their company* in the face of risk and beyond the actions expected in the role they occupy. Such heroes emerge in companies where innovation is open to everyone. I-heroes go beyond what their boss expects of them; they see and create from unknown or overlooked opportunities and then commit their personal energy to making their innovation successful in the marketplace. This is profound because innovation myths are about universal human desires and conflicts driven by the emotional drives to create, learn, and dream.

Morong's work (1992) traces the similarities between heroes and entrepreneurs. If we generalize his work to innovators in companies, we see startling similarities between classical heroes and I-heroes. First, both heroes and innovators are "called" to adventure. There is a discovery. There is a period of "fabulous forces" when the innovation team tinkers and conjures up a product or service. Heroes and innovators bring change. Morong notes common personality traits of people who create change, including creativity and the propensity for taking risks. I-heroes master these traits in the workplace and use them to present a solution onto the world. I-heroes follow their passion and, in the process, help revitalize the business. Morong suggests that this inspiration to answer the call moves people from being consumers to being producers or creators. Innovators are "called" to take part in universal adventures that include self-discovery and personal creativity.

In light of embedded innovation, Morong makes a serendipitous assertion. It is *mentors* who guide both heroes and innovators. Mentors help I-heroes slay their fear of the unknown to discover their creative ability. I-mentors at Whirlpool certainly fill this role; armed with the knowledge they have gained through their experience of having gone through the process before and the set of tools to help the innovators, I-mentors serve as an I-hero's guide.

Recognizing Potential I-Heroes

Although management cannot create I-heroes, it is useful to understand what potential I-heroes look like. They are not usually the charismatic, fast-track up-and-comers to whom management pays the most attention. In fact, they are often hard to spot. There are many sources of I-heroes, but four types come to the surface when innovation is open to everyone: the searchers, the orphans and outcasts, the thrill seekers, and the rebels.

The Searchers

Many people who become I-heroes are searchers at heart, passionately searching internally for sparks of excitement but also externally to help others and to gain recognition more than money. Campbell (1969) described how the hero's fever of passion eclipses money and material things. Searchers embark on the hero's journey because they choose to, even if they are reluctant at first. Along the way, they make profound choices and exercise their free will to surmount challenges.

I-heroes who follow their passion unlock their creativity to fulfill their need to be innovative. Through learning and creating new knowledge, they enhance themselves and others who benefit from their experiences. Searchers learn, grow, and perhaps gain notoriety; they contribute to society by solving vexing problems. Do you know a searcher in your company? Chances are that you don't, because searchers are unassuming. They are often wrongly cast in their day job. They are intellectually restless without much external evidence of their internal struggle; they are smart and insightful, but overlooked and often worn down by monotony. Imagine what searchers could do if innovation attracted them. Searchers are the archetype of the hero of embedded innovation: prolific dreamers who are capable of greatness but wrongly cast.

The Orphans and Outcasts

According to Gilder (1984), an expert on entrepreneurs, orphans and outcasts carry out innovations. There are orphans and outcasts in all organizations, people who sit on the fringes and never fully commit or "drink the Kool-Aid." You can tell who they are; they smirk at the company meeting when they hear corporate-speak, and make Dilbert-like observations. Orphans and outcasts are good innovators because they can see company orthodoxies that others cannot. They rebel against established practices and defect from the norm. Perhaps this is why embedded innovation that is open to everyone attracts the people to whom no one pays attention, the outcasts who have been marginalized by the organization. They are an unlikely and uncomfortable set of I-heroes, because to innovate and receive acclaim presents them with a moral dilemma: the acclaim they desire is from the organization they are trying not to "join." They are more comfortable being acknowledged as the customer's hero, but we believe they also strive to be I-heroes within their company. When innovation is embedded, orphans and outcasts have the opportunity to rebel against orthodoxies and perhaps become I-heroes.

Thrill Seekers

Some I-heroes are thrill seekers, craving the rush of adrenaline that comes with dangerous pursuits. They enjoy looking where no one else is looking—living on the edge, seeing just how far they can go. They are on a journey or quest for new experiences in places no one has gone before. Thrill seekers like the unknown and enjoy putting their structure around the white space of innovation to put forth their unique answer. As a team, they are inextricably bound together by their quest. Embedded innovation can take I-heroes to places that they would not ordinarily go, a thrill seeker's dream. I-heroes know that innovation is a passport to new and thrilling places.

Rebels

People that have a rebel streak are good candidates for being I-heroes. When they join a company, their rebellious and irreverent side is still there, but they camouflage it. Embedded innovation benefits from I-heroes who rebel against the norm, against standard-issue and routine competitor offerings. Innovation demands irreverence to see things differently, and often it is the rebel who can see different perspectives. Remember the Inspired Chef group we mentioned in Chapter Two, who, in summarizing what they had learned about what it took to innovate successfully, wrote in one of their presentations, "Don't become distracted by appeasing the corporate 'gods.'" The rebel is driven to innovation and is often a leading contender for I-hero status.

As these four types show, people who become I-heroes are not "well adjusted." They have interests other than moving smoothly up the corporate ladder. They do not fit in. They may be seen as disruptive, as loners, dreamers, even nuisances. Yet they are invaluable to embedded innovation, often producing innovation gold.

All of the examples of innovators in this book speak to a personal drive and a force that to others is not "normal" and is therefore greatly admired. Even at Whirlpool, where innovating should be relatively easy, the environment resists innovations, and I-heroes emerge because they are resistance fighters. Attainment of I-hero status at Whirlpool is not any easier than in many companies and is equally unpredictable.

What I-Heroes Seek

Embedded innovation offers a unique environment for the mythology of I-heroes to emerge. It is not a panacea, but embedded innovation offers the possibility of fulfillment of a handful of individual needs that are increasingly hard to satisfy in traditional work settings and even in settings outside of work. These include identity and accomplishment, recognition and acclaim, impact and legacy, meaning and higher purpose.

Identity and Accomplishment

For many people, the workplace is one of only a few places where they can find growth and fulfillment. Csikszentmihalyi (2003), a teacher at the Peter F. Drucker School of Management, found that many people enjoy their job and are fulfilled at work when they find a balance between opportunities to distinguish themselves and ways to contribute to the overarching vision of their organization. These moments of balance, when we become completely engrossed in the joy and excitement of work, are rare, however. For innovators, this is the period of idea forming and problem solving where the "aha" happens. I-heroes live for this moment and know that it is fleeting and rare, making it all the more precious.

Recognition and Acclaim

According to Parnaby and Sacco (2004), recognition and fame exist on a continuum. At the left of the continuum is fame, meaning a public reputation that is increasingly independent of accomplishment and seen as self-serving. In today's world of media saturation, there are people who are famous for being famous. Recognition is in the middle of the continuum as an acknowledgment that suggests approval. All the way to the right of the continuum is acclaim, the enthusiastic broad approval usually associated with great accomplishment. I-heroes seek acclaim. Parnaby and Sacco suggest that in some cultures the desire to be acclaimed parallels the imperative of achieving personal economic success. Organizations offer few meaningful ways to recognize contributions and rarely offer acclaim to people below C-level executives. Many organizations restrict acclaim to a few top leaders, but those with embedded innovation remove the restriction.

Impact and Legacy

In 1968, a short film about human creativity won the Academy Award. *Why Man Creates*, by Saul Bass and Mayo Simon, is as provocative as its title suggests. The film looks at creation throughout the ages and uncovers the essence of why humans need to create. The film beautifully asserts that there is a strong human tendency in each of us to look inward at ourselves and outward at our world to make sense of our existence and to create lasting impact on our community or society. The film ends with a profound proclamation: "Yet among all the variety of human expression, a thread of connection, a common mark can be seen. The urge to look into one's self, out at the world and say, 'I am unique, I am here, I am'" (Bass and Bass, 1968).

The profoundness of this expression of self is hard to translate into a traditional work setting. Yet many of us spend more time and energy at work than we do in any other part of our life. It is a sad commentary that we don't have an opportunity during a major part of our lives to express one of the most basic human needs, to create. I-heroes are searching for impact and legacy, but not in contrived ways. They know that one of the best ways to leave a legacy is through innovation. Leaving a legacy is important not just for CEOs but for each of us. I-heroes see their creations as one way to have impact and leave a legacy.

Meaning and Higher Purpose

Each of us needs a sense of meaning and to feel that the work we are doing is important and leading to the greater good. I-heroes see innovations as important solutions that are meaningful to customers and that contribute to the success of the company. This avenue to higher purpose through innovation seems to go beyond "doing your job really well." I-heroes use innovation to fast-track their results to have an impact on the organization, the market, and customers.

Connections with Other Emotional Drivers

Heroes and the need to create have deep connections. Morong (1994) states that "attaining the joy of being a creative, spiritually fulfilled person is probably the best thing we can do for

**Figure 11.1 Intersections of Emotional Drivers
of Embedded Innovation: Heroes**

Dream	Create	Heroes	Spirit
• Accelerating learning through dreams • Learning to use dreams	• Creating new knowledge • Learning valuable and fun tools	• **Fulfilling a journey of self-discovery** • **Forming ideas and problem solving**	• Creating a learning organization
	• Dreaming of possibilities	• **Fulfilling dream of new identity** • **Following dreams to self-fulfillment**	• Creating esprit de corps through group dreams
		• Unlocking creativity • Creating more heroes	• Engaging and attracting potential innovators
			• **Revitalizing the organization** • **Creating mythology and cultural norms**

Learn (row 1), *Dream* (row 2), *Create* (row 3), *Heroes* (row 4)

ourselves" (p. 5). Heroes and innovators are called to take part in a great universal adventure that is a journey of self-discovery, growth, and creativity. The connections between I-heroes and dreaming, creating, and learning are undeniable (see Figure 11.1). The hero's journey is one of self-discovery and problem solving. I-heroes and their mythology change culture. Stories of their success run rampant in organizations. In essence, I-heroes and what they stand for can revitalize an enterprise.

I-Heroes Are Mythical Creatures

A few years ago, Whirlpool North America decided to hold an innovation fair. We rented the local mall (there is only one) and invited about twenty innovation teams to set up a booth to display their innovations. Although we invited the press and local community, we created the fair for the people of Whirlpool to learn about and become interested in innovation. We invited three thousand Whirlpool people who worked in or near the North American headquarters. We chartered and ran buses from the headquarters to the mall to make it easy for everyone to attend. People showed up in droves. The event was a huge success for many reasons, but the most important was that it created a mythology around the innovators. The mall I-heroes were everyday people doing everyday jobs, with one exception: they answered the call and now were receiving public acclaim for their innovation. People at Whirlpool still talk about the fair with great reverence. Our collective memory of the fair focuses not on the innovations, creative as they were, but on the innovators who pitched their innovations to their colleagues with pride and passion. In our collective memory is a special feeling about the mall I-heroes. The fair is now part of the Whirlpool mythology.

If you could, you would create I-heroes, thousands of them. But as we noted at the outset of this chapter, they are not made by you; they emerge from the best within each of us and the right organizational environment. They are mythical. They are what is most virtuous in embedded innovation. I-heroes attract new innovators. They attract new talent to your company. Word gets out. Potential employees want to work for a company where they have a chance to innovate. Showing them the I-pipe will not attract them, but telling them about the I-heroes will. With success comes a few phone calls from the business press. Answer those calls and ask the reporters to talk to your I-heroes.

Eventually, top talent in the world will begin to read about your I-heroes. When they come to interview at your company, they will ask every interviewer about the I-heroes and find that I-heroes are credible and real. Word gets out. Fire your recruiting department and send out I-heroes. Ask them to speak at lunch meetings and at college recruiting events, or to write for the corporate newsletter. Call on your I-heroes to help new innovators and to meet with new employees. Ask for their help. I-heroes are the best and most underutilized asset in attracting talent, both internal and external. Many of them are happy to do it; they became innovators to help others and for the reward and recognition that might follow. They will love the acclaim they receive for helping the company in ways even they could not imagine.

Change management does not change culture as well as stories and folklore can. The mythology of I-heroes will grow, and so will the legend. I-heroes alone will not be sufficient for a culture of innovation to succeed, but they are a catalyst that is hard to match. With such heroes, the culture will shift in favor of innovation. Keeping that culture change going in the right direction is dependent on the rational framework for innovation and its utility to innovators and I-heroes. You will need to keep working on the rational drivers to allow the emotional drivers to surface. The two types of drivers work in symbiosis.

It takes wisdom to know that you cannot create these mythical I-heroes. You are not in control of their destiny. It takes wisdom and visionary leadership to accept this dynamic and instead to create an innovation environment that unleashes the *possibility* of I-heroes and, in so doing, revitalizes your company.

12

SPIRIT

Morale is the state of mind. It is steadfastness and
courage and hope. It is confidence and zeal and
loyalty. It is élan, esprit de corps and determination.
—*General George Catlett Marshall*

Innovation is not pursued for its own sake at Whirlpool; it is a means to an end: providing us with a sustainable competitive advantage. We want to win in the marketplace. The spirit of winning is what drives us to innovate. Although we discuss it as the final emotional driver, spirit—particularly the spirit of winning—is really the primary emotional driver of embedded innovation. The spirit of winning more than anything else led us to embed innovation in the first place.

Spirit is a life force—we speak of a winning spirit, a team spirit, a spirited conversation, a spirit inside that animates us. People who are full of spirit are enthusiastic and full of life; they have a can-do attitude. And in a deeper sense, we are spiritual beings, seeking out meaning, yearning for spiritual fulfillment. Spirit is perhaps the most profound yet elusive emotional driver.

If you are uncomfortable with the term *spirit*, you might prefer the concept of engagement, which has gotten an enormous amount of attention in the last few years. Engagement and spirit are closely related. On the job, spirit becomes engagement. We will talk specifically about engagement later in the chapter. For now, we want to focus on spirit, which we think goes a little deeper than engagement.

Spirit is the ultimate input and output of embedded innovation because creation, innovation, and being part of something bigger than ourselves that is positive and community oriented are related to our true anima or energy as humans and are primary needs. Finding something that fulfills those needs is often more difficult in the workplace than in our personal life. For many at Whirlpool, embedded innovation provides the opportunity to contribute in a way that is fundamentally fulfilling. In this chapter, we show how the spirit of winning drives innovation, examine four factors that sustain the competitive spirit required for winning, and show how spirit translates into employee engagement—detailing the three most important factors for promoting engagement.

The Spirit of Winning

Spirit is the pride of creating, winning, and being part of a process that is energetic and courageous. Whirlpool's values include a value called "Spirit of Winning," which is described as follows:

> It begins with the belief that setting and achieving ambitious goals is key to extraordinary performance. Sticking to the status quo, or being just a little better than last year, is not good enough. There is no room for the "fear of failure." Whirlpool's culture and values will enable individuals and teams to appropriately reach and take pride in extraordinary results and further inspire the Spirit of Winning in all of us.
>
> In the Spirit of Winning culture, everyone is a leader, responsible for his or her own actions. With a full awareness and understanding of Whirlpool's strategic aims, these individual and team actions will drive outstanding performance.

Why do people like to win, and what are the characteristics of winners? Do these characteristics have to do with winning itself or with the creation and sustaining of spirit? In the process of embedding innovation, we learned that giving people an outlet for creativity and innovation and a way to compete might actually bring forth the characteristics of winners—and, in the process, create spirit.

Patrick Cohn, a sports psychologist, is cited in *USA Today* suggesting that elite athletes have a set of four characteristics in common: competitiveness, confidence, composure, and focus (Brady, 2006). We believe that there is a great deal in common between a competitive or winning spirit in sports and such a spirit in the business world, and that these four qualities are important in sustaining spirit in either realm.

Competitiveness

Top athletes love the heat of battle, according to Cohn (Brady, 2006). "They're motivated by testing their skills against the next person. Obviously, they love to win and hate to lose. You need that. People might think, 'Well, isn't everyone competitive?' The answer is 'no.' The really competitive person digs deeper than the next person."

Innovation in a corporation is all about competitive advantage. Embedded innovation from everyone and everywhere provides Whirlpool and its people with another mechanism for winning in the marketplace. And it is working; Whirlpool has been rated as one of the most innovative companies in the world by a variety of sources, and that reputation has fueled sales, shareholder value, and pride. Our competitive spirit was especially apparent in the grueling early years of embedded innovation, when we were far from the breakthrough point on the S-curve. Although successes were few and far between in those early years, our competitive spirit, our desire to win, kept us going.

Confidence

"Self-confidence is probably the No. 1 mental skill that championship athletes possess," Cohn (Brady, 2006) says. "Simply put, it is their belief in their ability to perform. They see themselves as winners. They think, act and behave in very confident ways."

According to Harvard Business School professor Rosabeth Moss Kanter (2006), building confidence is a key responsibility of leaders. "Leaders must deliver confidence at every level: self-confidence, confidence in each other, confidence in the system, and the confidence of external investors and the public that their support is warranted. Leaders create organizations and cultures that develop confidence in advance of victory, in order to attract the investments that make victory possible—money, talent, support, loyalty, attention, effort, or people's best thinking" (p. 56).

Confidence breeds success, and success enhances confidence. At Whirlpool, our decision to seek innovation from everyone and everywhere was based on our confidence in ourselves and all our people. We would never have embarked on this company-changing effort had we lacked confidence in our ultimate success. In addition, learning and applying innovation tools has boosted many people's confidence in their ability not only to learn a new tool set but to apply it toward creating value for the company, their workgroup, and, in some cases, the community. For many, just the notion that innovation could come from any-one, anywhere built confidence that being creative and innova-tive is not just the purview of senior management. The results of Whirlpool's innovation efforts have also given the company and the people in it confidence in their ability to innovate on a repeated basis.

Composure

According to Cohn (Brady, 2006), composure has two aspects: how well you handle pressure and how you deal with mistakes. "The first is: Can you keep it together under pressure at crunch time? It's the last minute of the game, and you're trailing by three: It's how well you can stay under control emotionally and can perform when you need to. The other component is how well you deal with mistakes. Can you stay composed and forget about them? Or do you get upset and frustrated and thrown off your game? Athletes who are composed don't get rattled and compound one mistake into many."

Composure was especially important at Whirlpool during the early days of the effort to embed innovation. Every quarter, I had a performance appraisal review with Jeff Fettig. If you have seen the movie *Groundhog Day*, you will understand what these meetings were like. Each quarter we met during that period, he said the same thing: "Nancy, I like what I am seeing in innovation; I see a lot of good progress. But I do not see results that equate with the investment we have made in innovation. At some point we need to start getting the results from the big investment we have put into innovation, or this will not succeed. We need to scale it." I felt as if I were in a loop that I could not escape. It was the dark period of the S-curve that many innovation architects experience, the period before breakthrough. These were trying times, but we managed to keep our composure. By definition, innovation involves attempting new things and going through a period of trial and error. If you have spirit, you can stay composed through the inevitable setbacks. We finally broke out of the loop and hit the tipping point.

In addition, companies can help build composure by having a specific methodology, set of tools, and supporting processes and systems that help people innovate. Athletes gain composure from years and years of practice. Similarly, the structure and processes of embedded innovation, including experimentation and market tests, serve as the practice and the playing field for people to build not only confidence but also composure in innovation. Further, because the process of embedded innovation expects setbacks, mistakes, and diversions, people don't feel as if a failed or shelved innovation project reflects on them. They are able to maintain composure through both good and not so productive times.

Focus

The ability to stay focused on important goals and not be distracted is critical in both sports and business. "The idea is to give focus and attention to what's most important—and, when you do get distracted, to refocus quickly," Cohn says (Brady, 2006). "This is the key component to success in sports such as gymnastics and diving, but it's important in all sports."

During those early days of seeking innovation from everyone and everywhere, when progress was slow, focus was critically important. We kept our eyes on the long-term goal of embedding innovation and didn't get distracted by setbacks or by the pursuit of quick hits. In turn, as embedded innovation took hold, it brought focus to Whirlpool's strategy and collective energy. It provided a collective identity and target for competitive drive and spirit that everyone could agree on and rally around. We don't have hard evidence for this, but we submit that it is much more difficult to have spirit around cost and quality focuses, as compared to a focus on something freeing and creative, such as innovation.

Drawing on our competitive instincts and giving us the confidence, composure, and focus we needed, the embedded innovation effort has helped make our value of the Spirit of Winning come alive, much in the way that a good game plan makes a good team even more competitive. Embedded innovation engages everyone who is interested in winning. It eliminates the "bench," if you will, and makes everyone a player.

The Spirit of Engagement

Another word for spirit that is more commonly used in the workplace is engagement, as we noted earlier. When people are truly engaged in an activity, they say they feel more alive. They show and embody the anima and vigor that are essential to spirit. Much has been written lately about employee engagement. According to Welbourne (2007), employee engagement is one of the "hottest topics in management. Everyone seems to be on the path to getting their employees engaged" (p. 45). The Gallup organization (2007), which has conducted extensive surveys on employee engagement, defines engaged employees as those who work with passion and feel a profound connection to their company. Employees who are not engaged go through the motions, but they are essentially sleepwalking through the workday.

And research shows that engagement matters. For example, a recent study by Towers Perrin found that companies with the highest levels of employee engagement achieve better financial results and are more successful in retaining their most valued employees than companies with lower levels of engagement. Unfortunately, Towers Perrin also found that just 21 percent of the employees surveyed around the world are engaged in their work ("Towers Perrin Study Finds Significant 'Engagement Gap' Among Global Workforce," 2007).

Moreover, Gallup's research demonstrates that engagement is directly connected to innovation. Its research indicates that workplace engagement is a powerful factor in catalyzing outside-the-box thinking to improve management and business processes as well as customer service. Gallup also found that 59 percent of engaged employees strongly agreed with the statement that their current job "brings out [their] most creative ideas." On the flip side, only 17 percent of unengaged and just 3 percent of actively disengaged employees strongly agreed with that statement.

The bottom line is that organizations are finding that employees who are engaged are more productive, are absent and sick less often, are more loyal to the company and less likely to leave, and are more creative than employees who are not "engaged."

The way Whirlpool uses the term *engagement* implies three outcomes. The first is that people are putting in some sort of discretionary effort in their jobs, not because they have to or are required to, but because they want to. It is important to recognize that Whirlpool does not "require" discretionary effort above and beyond what it normally takes to do an excellent job. We value family time and time for self. However, we also value the extent to which people feel engaged and excited enough to feel a higher level of energy and excitement about their job. The second outcome is that people are loyal to Whirlpool. That is, when people are engaged, they are less likely to seek employment elsewhere and are more likely to see Whirlpool as a place where they will weather the ups and downs of normal business cycles. The third outcome is that people act as champions for the customer.

Factors That Promote Engagement

Whirlpool found that there were three main categories that help promote the three engagement outcomes: great jobs, great leaders, and an inclusive environment.

Great Jobs

It is hard to be engaged if you are stuck in an ill-defined or poorly conceived job. Great jobs are those that are considered meaningful by the people in them, in that they make a positive and visible contribution to Whirlpool's success. These are also jobs that demand a wide variety of people's skills and abilities, enabling them to continue learning and growing. People with spirit rise to challenges, and great jobs provide meaningful challenges.

Embedded innovation at Whirlpool helps everyone have access to a great job, in that innovation can be a challenging and meaningful component of *every* job. People who are I-mentors or who have participated in innovation activities and have learned the innovation tools and techniques tell us that innovation has helped make their jobs more meaningful and that the education in and use of the innovation tools has given them an avenue for development that they might not have had access to otherwise. Many I-mentors, as cited in Chapter Six, recall that the innovation effort gave them something bigger than themselves to focus on. It also provided them with a broader range of skills with which to make a difference inside the company and in community activities.

Innovation training has also given many a higher degree of business acumen: through their learning about how to translate innovations and experiments into profitable activities, innovators gained a direct "line of sight" into how their work contributed to Whirlpool's success. Innovation training also provided a mechanism for people's competitive spirit to play out by allowing them to understand how business metrics are tracked and measured against competition.

Great Leaders

These are individuals who others willingly follow and who care about people and their development as well as the goals of the company. Welbourne (2007) notes that at many companies, unfortunately, "leaders are creating or are in an environment where employee engagement will be very difficult to achieve" (p. 49). She says that any systematic approach to employee engagement needs to start at the top, with the leadership team. Leaders who are not engaged themselves will have a difficult time engaging those who work for them.

We have found that the tools and techniques of embedded innovation serve as an additional set of methods enabling people to be great leaders—that is, effective in driving others' activities toward goals that support the success not only of the company but also of individuals, in terms of their own growth and learning.

Whirlpool leaders are able to use embedded innovation to promote the spirit of winning in many different ways.

Innovation itself gives leaders something everyone can rally around—against competitors, rather than against each other in the petty infighting that often marks mature companies. Innovation has had untold benefits in terms of focusing competitive energy on a set of company-wide metrics that tell a story of success against the competition.

The success of innovation has also given leaders within Whirlpool the confidence to take more risks and know that they are able to win the marketplace with managed innovation. This confidence has helped develop a set of leaders and a culture at Whirlpool that is forward looking and open to new ideas. Leaders have learned how to foster an environment where new ideas are welcome and innovation and creativity are valued.

This is a marked change from how we described the culture of Whirlpool before the innovation effort began: as a culture that was completely risk averse and where anyone could say no.

Inclusive Environment

The final requirement for engagement is an inclusive environment. No one will feel engaged in an environment that does not welcome his or her ideas and participation. Full engagement, of everyone from everywhere, requires an environment that values and respects diversity of thought and ideas and fosters participation. We noted in Chapter Ten how important diversity and inclusion are for creativity. Because embedded innovation, by definition, comes from everyone and everywhere, it embodies an inclusive environment. Because any employee can, if he wants to, become involved in an innovation effort as an I-mentor or innovation team member, or by using innovation tools in his everyday job, no one is excluded from the innovation effort.

On an innovation team, it does not matter where an idea comes from, as long as it works. Beating the competition entails going beyond the standard ways of doing business, and as we noted in Chapter Ten, teams with more diverse membership appear to have the power to create more creative and innovative ideas that win in the marketplace than do teams with a more uniform composition. Diversity of thought and ideas is clearly a powerful driver of innovation.

Further, learning innovation tools and participating on innovation teams give people from diverse backgrounds and experiences the tools, skills, and successes to have confidence and composure in a number of other business situations. In other words, people's experiences with innovation build a generalized sense of confidence that goes beyond knowledge and skills in a specific discipline. Innovation activities also give individuals who might not be used to working in environments with diverse team members a set of positive and productive experiences that generalize to other workplace activities.

Embedded Innovation Lights the Spark

Spirit has a deep connection with the other emotional drivers, as shown in Figure 12.1. The spirit of innovation helps create a learning organization and it also enables teams of people to dream. It attracts potential innovators, both inside and outside the company. Through thousands of hero's journeys, the organization is revitalized, and new cultural norms are created.

As humans, we all have an inherent need for challenge, growth, learning, and accomplishment. Embedded innovation offers the opportunity for individuals from all parts of the corporation to participate in activities that allow them not only to grow and develop but also to take part in contributing to the company's competitiveness and success.

Embedded innovation builds spirit because it provides a focus for activities across the company that light the spark of engagement. It targets everyone's competitive drive toward beating the competition, not each other, focusing people on activities that have the potential to add value to the company.

Figure 12.1 Intersections of Emotional Drivers of Embedded Innovation: Spirit

Dream	Create	Heroes	Spirit
• Accelerating learning through dreams • Learning to use dreams	• Creating new knowledge • Learning valuable and fun tools	• Fulfilling a journey of self-discovery • Forming ideas and problem solving	• Creating a learning organization
	• Dreaming of possibilities	• Fulfilling dream of new identity • Following dreams to self-fulfillment	• Creating esprit de corps through group dreams
		• Unlocking creativity • Creating more heroes	• Engaging and attracting potential innovators
			• Revitalizing the organization • Creating mythology and cultural norms

Learn (arrow) — row 1
Dream (arrow) — row 2
Create (arrow) — row 3
Heroes (arrow) — row 4

Further, it builds engagement through its potential to make all jobs great jobs; by giving leaders confidence and a set of tools that focus everyone's attention on winning; and by fostering an inclusive environment where everyone has the opportunity to participate on a winning team.

Conclusion

THE INNOVATION JOURNEY

As we write the conclusion to this book, it strikes us that we can never really write the conclusion to the story it tells. Whirlpool has reached a tipping point where innovation is a right of every person—and each is supported by a machine that creates and nurtures innovations. We have managed to structure our vision, management systems, innovation processes, and people skills to get results in the marketplace. We have harnessed the energy and emotions of the people at Whirlpool to embrace innovation at work and in the community. But as far as we have come, we feel that our innovation journey is just beginning. Innovation will continue to evolve and take us to places we never expected.

Lessons of Embedded Innovation

As we look back at how far we have come and forward to the exciting possibilities, we have three big take-away lessons, beyond the details of how to embed innovation that are contained in the chapters of this book: (1) that the interplay between the rational drivers and the emotional drivers of innovation is critical to embedment; (2) that these innovation drivers create a culture that sustains innovation; and (3) that to sustain innovation, constant adaptation—flexibility combined with perseverance—is required, and this only happens through leadership that stays the course.

The Interplay Between the Rational and the Emotional Is Critical

Embedded innovation is an approach that Whirlpool pioneered to entice innovation from everywhere and everyone. As we noted in the Introduction, embedding innovations requires a thoroughgoing restructuring of systems and procedures and a strong focus on the hearts and minds of the people who ultimately create innovations. Embedded innovation creates sustainable and differentiated business results by enabling innovation from the rational framework of the business while creating an environment that sanctions and reclaims our human need to create. The rational drivers include the strategic architecture, management systems, the I-pipe, innovators and I-mentors, and managing execution and results. The emotional drivers include learning, dreaming, creating, the mythology of heroes, and the spirit of winning. It is the virtual system that rational and emotional drivers create that makes embedded innovation so unique and compelling.

Like a human body, embedded innovation needs a skeletal system and muscles that hold it upright. The strategic architecture is like the skeleton that gives the effort form and direction. This is key to setting the stage for innovation and to ensuring that the effort is aligned with the vision of the company. Management systems and tracking mechanisms, such as the I-pipe, function as muscles. They keep innovation on track and headed toward desired outcomes. I-mentors who embrace and use innovation techniques act as ambassadors and provide the lifeblood for embedded innovation. Without them, all the management and tracking systems in the world cannot execute the effort or yield results.

A human being is more than the body, however: we have minds that yearn to learn and create, and a spirit that dreams of heroic exploits. Our human need to continually learn, create, dream, become heroes, and feel the spirit of winning are what truly drives innovation during the good times and the bad. Tapping into and honoring these needs are critical for any human being and are essential for innovation to be embedded and to create results.

As we noted in Chapter Two, the emotional drivers have become embedded in our language, in new practices that have become second nature, and in the way we work together to innovate for our customers. And as we also noted, management cannot create the emotional drivers; they are already within each of us and can only be unleashed. Unfortunately, many companies have stifled their people's emotional drivers through years of command-and-control management, zero-variance initiatives, or excessive bureaucracy. Embedded innovation has allowed Whirlpool to begin to charter a course that taps into the emotional drivers of everyone, everywhere.

Innovation Creates a New Culture

Culture is created by taking what works and making it habitual to the point where people do not question the new practices. At Whirlpool, we knew that we did not have a culture that supported innovation when we began. It was not until we let go of the notion that we needed to change the culture through a direct cultural initiative, and instead worked to implement a direct innovation initiative, that we ultimately changed the culture.

As Frances Hesselbein, who led the transformation of the Girl Scouts of the USA, wrote,

> In times of great change, organizational culture gets special attention. Leaders issue calls for cultural change, stating: "We need a more entrepreneurial culture," or, "We must create a culture of accountability." If we could alter the underlying beliefs of our organizations, the thinking goes, our practices would surely follow.

But changing the culture of an organization requires a transformation of the organization itself—its purpose, its focus on customers and results. Culture does not change because we desire to change it. Culture changes when the organization is transformed; the culture reflects the realities of people working together every day. . . .

If we note Peter Drucker's definition of innovation—"change that creates a new dimension of performance"—it is the performance that changes the culture—not the reverse [1999, p. 6].

Our experience at Whirlpool showed us the truth of Hesselbein's observation. Over time we noticed that the sheer act of engaging in innovation activities required people to try out new and different behaviors and throw away some of the assumptions and practices that had defined our culture in the past. Managers became more willing to take risks, share resources, embrace diverse opinions and options, and let their people go for periods of time to work in other organizations. These were all things that we had tried to change before the innovation effort began, with minimal success. The innovation activities themselves required people to act in new ways that worked, and that is what finally changed the culture.

The lesson is that culture changes through actions that work and that can be seen and adopted by the collective. The way to create a culture that supports innovation is to innovate; waiting until the culture is ripe for innovation is most likely a losing proposition.

Flexible and Committed Leadership Is Key

One of the critical success factors for embedding innovation is the ability to stay the course. It helps to have a leader at the top and a cadre of senior leaders who are committed to see the effort through.

Just as important, responsible leaders take succession planning seriously so that a leadership transition does not disrupt the organization. When Dave Whitwam retired, he ensured that the person who took the helm was like-minded about not only the innovation effort but also other corporate and strategic initiatives. Although we can't say what might have happened without this consistency of purpose in the senior person, it is obvious that the senior person in any organization sets the direction of strategic initiatives such as innovation. Because our innovation effort was a multiyear activity with many twists and turns, success required someone who was not going to change direction at the first sign of trouble. For Dave Whitwam, Jeff Fettig was that person.

It is common knowledge that change efforts in large and established organizations take between five and ten years. If your organization is not committed to that time frame and unwilling to wait several years for results, our advice would be, don't even try. Our experience is that embedded innovation is a very long-term effort that requires long-term commitment *and* a high degree of flexibility and adaptability.

The details of the innovation effort at Whirlpool today look very different from when we started. We have gone through many revisions to the methods that we use to better understand the customer, leading to increasing innovation revenue.

Any long-term change effort, whether focused on innovation or on anything else, needs a magnetic north to guide it. In our case, this was a complete focus on our customers' needs and wants and the mantra that innovation is possible from anyone, anywhere. However, the effort needs to be flexible and adaptable enough to change with the external environment. Keeping this balance between a steady direction and flexibility has to be modeled by senior leaders.

A Long Way to Go

When we began our innovation effort, we never could have imagined its results—for Whirlpool; for our people, customers, and shareholders; and for the communities in which we live and work. Embedded innovation needs to be constantly focused on our customers and business results. We knew this going in. What we have learned is that this type of activity can also change the lives of our leaders, employees, and communities, as you will discover in the Epilogue.

Innovation at Whirlpool still has a long way to go. We are perpetually dissatisfied, and we continue to learn more and more about embedding innovation. There were times while we were writing this book that the innovation effort at Whirlpool skyrocketed and times when we wondered if it would rise to the next set of challenges. But we are confident now that innovation has a life of its own and will continue to take us into new and exciting territory.

Epilogue

DRAGONS BE HERE

Never doubt that a small group of committed
people can change the world. Indeed, it is the only
thing that ever has.

—*Margaret Mead*

Whirlpool has a history of going into unexplored spaces. "Dragons Be Here" is the phrase that old-world mapmakers put on the edges of their maps to suggest unexplored territories. It was also the title of a seminal speech Dave Whitwam made in 1988 to globalize Whirlpool when the appliance industry was locally entrenched. Although he mentions innovation in the speech, the speech predates the embedded innovation transformation by more than a decade. Nearly twenty years after he spoke them, I am still struck by what his words have to say about Whirlpool, embedded innovation, and Whitwam himself:

> In each country, mapmakers provided extensive detail, painstakingly illustrated, for the area inside the region's borders . . . the 'known' world, the comfortable world viewed with an eye to the past. But away from these familiar environs their only comment was a dire warning. 'Dragons be here,' they wrote. . . . After all, only a fool would choose dragons over the comfortable, secure familiarity of home, of the way things were. And so it remained . . . until there arose people of vision and ambition and purpose, people who braved the dragons for the unknown, people who reached excellence and hungered to define the universe in their own terms, managing their own change. And who, in doing so, won an entire new world.

He ended by saying, "And I promise you one more thing: our experiences will be built on pure excitement and sheer fun . . . as we shun the dragons of the unknown."

The speech has remained in Whirlpool's collective memory as a call to conquer unknown spaces. Innovation became one of these unknown spaces. It is only with perfect 20/20 hindsight that we can see what the speech foreshadowed. Whirlpool started embedded innovation in 1999 with bold ideas deeply rooted in the belief that people in every walk of life can innovate. In many ways, Whitwam was ahead of his time.

From the vision of Whitwam and under the leadership of Fettig, the exploration continues. The innovators at Whirlpool took the vision of innovation from everywhere and everyone "at its word." Innovation from everyone and everywhere was like a passport that allowed people to travel to places that not even Whitwam could have foreseen. Embedded innovation from everywhere and everyone is without limits. When innovation is truly embedded, it is not embedded in systems: it is embedded in people. *There arose people of vision and purpose . . . who hungered to define the universe in their own terms, managing their own change . . . who won an entire new world.*

Transforming People, Organizations, and Communities

Embedded innovation is now occurring in many venues, but none more interesting and rewarding than in community service—and these efforts are transforming the people involved, the communities we serve, and Whirlpool itself. Many of the innovators of Whirlpool have volunteered to partner with community leaders and nonprofit members to apply innovation tools and processes to local government and nonprofit endeavors. They are helping community teams innovate by creating new frameworks of inclusive, community innovation while tapping into the social drivers of volunteerism. Facilitating innovation in the community is a serendipitous outcome when everyone is invited to innovate.

When we surveyed the I-mentors for this book, we asked them if they, or someone they knew, had used the tools outside Whirlpool in a nonprofit setting. We were surprised and amazed to read their responses. Not only were there numerous examples, but, as we interviewed a sample of the I-mentors on their community experiences, we found unparalleled pride and passion about their endeavors. The five examples we present here show how using innovation tools has helped people develop and gain self-confidence, strengthen outside community groups in many ways, and strengthen our internal community at Whirlpool.

Making a Contribution to Something Important

Carolina Mata-Tovar has been with Whirlpool for six years and has followed an interesting career path. She came to Whirlpool to work in corporate communications and became an I-mentor. She then was given a rare opportunity: to be a loaned executive to a community nonprofit organization. For over a year she worked in this organization, then returned to Whirlpool in a marketing capacity.

During her time as a loaned executive, Carolina was asked to facilitate an innovation ideation session with Habitat for Humanity International, headquartered in Americus, Georgia. Whirlpool has been a corporate sponsor with Habitat for Humanity since 1999 with an initial five-year, $25 million commitment. Habitat has a unique vision that proclaims that everyone on the planet deserves decent housing. In 2006, we expanded the partnership globally. Through our partnership, Whirlpool provides a range and refrigerator for every home built by Habitat. More important, in 2004 Whirlpool people volunteered over seven thousand hours during the workday, building more than 120 homes and helping improve the lives of thirty-six thousand families worldwide. Carolina's workshop participants were a cross-functional team of Habitat leadership. The workshop was a two-day event that used a variety of innovation tools to help Habitat create innovative streams of work that support their vision.

In the workshop, she helped the team look at their internal orthodoxies and how to overturn these to create an advantage. They also used an amended version of the customer benefit tools from innovation to look at examples of other organizations that have a world-class affiliate structure. And they used the innovation lens-smashing tools to create innovative streams about the housing industry, affiliate networks, and Habitat's core competencies. They created three work streams: strategic partnerships, activating the community, and the aftermarket for new homeowners.

We asked Carolina why the innovation tools and processes worked so well. With great pride and feeling of accomplishment, she told us, "The tools have a unique ability to align people's thinking and beliefs. They also help participants start a conversation to position their ideas into major innovative work streams. I think the innovation tools work as much for collaboration as for the actual idea generation. The Habitat group was very interested in trying to innovate and cared very much, but had no idea how to get started. Innovation tools helped them do that."

In explaining how the experience affected her, Carolina told us that facilitating innovation outside Whirlpool helped her learn about Whirlpool and her job. Habitat faced some of the same transformation challenges as Whirlpool. "It helps me get more out of my job." She also talked about how powerful the use of the orthodoxy tools was to the initiative. Upon reflection, she said that the orthodoxy process forces you to face up to your parochialism. "It hurts. I learned to say when we start the tool,

'You are not going to like me when we start working on ortho-doxies, but trust me, it will help.'" Her personal reflection and reason for facilitating this and other nonprofit innovation ses-sions is that "I love doing it and I love working with non-product innovation. It is so exciting to see the light bulbs come on. I feed off of that excitement and energy." She also said it gives her more self-confidence and a great deal of gratification when she works with nonprofit groups. "I feel like I am really making a contribu-tion to something important."

She closed our discussion by telling us, "Sometimes when I volunteer and I am really busy at work, I regret that I offered, especially as the meeting gets closer. But once it starts, it is so rewarding. I think the bottom line for me is that I feel like I am working on something meaningful, and I always learn some-thing new." At the time of our interview with her, Carolina was preparing to help with a second installment of innovation with Habitat. "They must have liked it; they invited me back!" she said with a huge smile.

Connecting to the Community

Barbara Rand is one of the most skillful I-mentors we know. The board of a small local symphony asked her to help them with some strategy work. The symphony is a volunteer organization that leads a professional orchestra of eighty musicians. The par-ticipants in the strategy workshop were from a variety of pro-fessional and community backgrounds and ranged in ages from forty to seventy-five.

Barbara used the innovation tools to tackle this challenge and believed that the innovation process worked very well. It helped the team think about the business processes they need to put in place so that there is some institutionalizing of knowl-edge as members come and go. It also helped them view them-selves not just as artists who performed, but as artists who run a business. When we asked Barbara what she learned, she said she met new people, did new things, and even started going to the symphony. "I lived here for five years, and this is the first time I felt connected to the community."

As a result of her work, Barbara was asked to join the board of the symphony as the VP of marketing, an appointment she held for two years. She said often people don't know how to get involved in community, and innovation skills can be a rich and rewarding avenue for involvement. There are many groups who need out-of-the-box thinking about ideas for their future. The innovation process is great for that.

Finding Bigger Ideas

JD Rapp was asked to facilitate a group of local community leaders and members who were deciding what to do with a valuable tract of land known as the Bluffside, adjacent to the shores of Lake Michigan. A few generous patrons donated the land to the city with the proviso that the city would come up with a compelling solution for how to use it that would benefit the community. The Bluffside group consisted of about twenty-five local residents, contributors, and community leaders.

JD was asked to help the group reach consensus on their ideas, but when he got there, the facilitation assignment changed. The leader of the group felt that they were not ready for consensus. He felt that their ideas were not "big enough": they needed to create bigger alternatives. JD quickly regrouped and used various visioning tools to help the group describe what they wanted the city and community to look like in the future. Once they generated ideas, he grouped them into themes. He was surprised by how rich and emotional their visions were. He then facilitated them through a set of the innovation tools to help them expand their ideas. He recalls a rich set of themes that included unity and overcoming community division, tourism to spark the local economy, and entertainment for local families.

JD felt that the session worked very well for expanding the group's thinking. When we asked him what he learned, he said he was amazed at the rich emotional connection that developed within the first few minutes. He was not used to that at Whirlpool. At work, he told us, you have to help people get rid of "all the problems of the day" before they can really innovate. This was not the case with the community group. He learned that sometimes groups need pushing to figure out their real problem. In this case, it was not reaching consensus but thinking outside the box.

Seeing People and Groups Grow Stronger

Lynn Holmgren's story shows that facilitating an innovation event in the community is not as easy as it sounds. Lynn worked with a local agency that challenged her facilitation from the first word. She recalled that the initiative was run by two leaders who had a command-and-control style. The innovation tools open the process to all voices, and at first the leaders did not like that. Also, she felt that she had to prove herself, especially at the start. Some of the group did not like strategic thinking and were resistant to change. In short, the team she was working with was dysfunctional. She worked with this team over a five-month period to bring them together. When we asked her what she learned about herself, she said she was a "frustrated teacher and entrepreneur at heart." She really likes learning new things by mentoring people through the process. Her greatest reward was to stick with it and to see this team progress from not getting traction to becoming a respected and dominant agency in the community. They made themselves prominent, and they changed many aspects of how they function. She said, "Any time you do something for your community, it gives you a great feeling. Even more than your everyday job, you can see changes in the people and the agencies. It is a bit like gardening . . . it gets greener when you water it."

Building a More Inclusive Community at Whirlpool

Whirlpool's founders in 1911 could not have foreseen the twenty-first-century disadvantage of attracting global talent to the small-town, Midwest shores of Lake Michigan. After all, Benton Harbor, where Whirlpool's headquarters is located, is over "100 miles from anywhere" if you are young, talented, and accustomed to the fast, diverse urban lifestyle of the twenty- and thirty-something generations. A job offer at Whirlpool presents a dilemma for some: exciting career opportunities at a global company located in a community that, although perfect for families and small-town living, may not be what a single twenty-something is looking for. Makini Nyanteh, Brian Snyder (no relation to me), Ben Wojcikiewicz, and Peter Lamberta changed that with the use of innovation to create differentiated lifestyle opportunities for young professionals.

In 2005, Makini was the diversity director for Whirlpool. Her boss gave her a challenging assignment: identify barriers to inclusion for diverse groups and help Whirlpool remove the barriers to attracting diverse talent to our community. Although Whirlpool had diversity networks representing the interests of African Americans, women, Asian Americans, gays and lesbians, Hispanics, and Indigenous Americans, to name a few, Makini was intrigued by a pattern of responses that did not fit neatly into any of these networks. She saw a set of barriers to inclusion that were shared by people of a certain age and unique to working and living in a small midwestern town. She met with Brian, Ben, and Peter and worked on identifying barriers perceived by people they termed "young professionals."

Makini and Brian were both I-mentors trained in innovation and thinking about possibilities. They designed a series of workshops that used the innovation tools to address the challenges facing young professionals. They started with the orthodoxies that the inclusion barriers represented. With the help of many people and focus groups, they identified a list of things young professionals would never say about working for Whirlpool. Then they overturned these to see what they could innovate to make Whirlpool more attractive to young professionals. They focused innovation on what is necessary to feel welcome and valued at Whirlpool and what could be done within two years to make Whirlpool an attractive place for young professionals. Using the point of view of a young professional, they identified a migration path with four areas of work:

- What is my business impact?
- How am I developing and growing in my career?
- What is the social scene?
- How is the community working for me in terms of being inviting and welcoming?

Makini and Brian created an elevator speech: "a work environment where young professionals are comfortable being themselves, do not encounter barriers to success, and are empowered to contribute to their fullest in creating loyal customers for life." They used the migration paths as a great visual tool for innovation to help teams put a language and structure around their ideas.

With lots of help from people like Mark McLane and Dave Binkley (head of diversity and head of human resources, respectively), they set up the Young Professionals Network, with Ben, Peter, and Brian as coleaders. They established five steering committees with lead roles for young professionals to fill: leader of communications and reputation, leader of development and retention, leader of community involvement, leader of customer loyalty, and leader of a great place to live and work. By the end of 2005, they had established the network and had an impressive list of accomplishments (see Exhibit E.1). They had developed the network (now branded as YP!), surveyed and attracted

Exhibit E.1 Accomplishments of the Young Professionals Network, 2005

2005 Accomplishments

† Developing the network
  - Charter drafted and approved by Office of Global Diversity
  - Pulse survey of Whirlpool Young Professionals

† Contributing to Whirlpool and the community
  - Recruiting initiatives
  - Intern management
  - Participation in other diversity networks
  - United Way Day of Caring
  - Angel Tree
  - Bridges to Digital Excellence
  - Berrien County Cancer Society
  - Attending city commission meetings
  - "Cool Cities " initiative

Alvin Hernandez, Lance Moore, Melissa Bulliss, Peter Dallepezze, Kerry White, Peter Lamberta, Jessica Egerton, Erin Smith, George Jones, Tamara Snyder, Kelley Smith, and Brian Snyder at United Way Day of Caring 2005

young professionals, and contributed to Whirlpool and the community by working on recruiting initiatives, intern management, and a host of community and city contributions.

Today YP! has over five hundred members. In 2007, the network was named "Young Innovator of the Year" by the *Western Michigan Business Review*, which said, "Using industry-leading Whirlpool innovation methodology, the group articulated a clear need within the company to provide a unified voice for young professionals, empower them to better engage with and improve their contributions to the company, and strengthen the company's talent pipeline." YP! became the go-to group for market research and community engagement and action, as well as a sounding board for ideas. YP! is a pool of energetic and dedicated people who innovate around the four areas of work. Today people at Whirlpool can't imagine what it was like before YP! was formed.

When we asked Makini, Brian, and Peter about the innovation tools, they said, "The process is a lot richer than brainstorming. Innovation offers a fun way to create a vision and strategy for new concepts and initiatives." They recalled the great emotion around the topic and suggested that the tools work because they do not have a built-in bias. They allow teams to work with an issue without going into a downward spiral—plunging into a negative or nonproductive place. Makini reflected that having "access to the suite of innovation tools gave me confidence that I was empowered with a skill set to achieve the task. When someone says to you, 'find the top two barriers to inclusion and help Whirlpool remove them,' this can seem daunting or overly simplistic. With innovation, I know that I was equipped with a process that was tested, proven, inclusive, creative and results-driven. I knew that I could find an answer." Brian said his experience using the tools "reinforced the idea that the innovation process is universally applicable for uncovering unarticulated needs and not limited to product development." He considers the tools fun and effective yet simultaneously powerful and simple enough to engage participation without much instruction.

These are just five stories of how innovation embeds itself in people who learn and use the tools, and then, through those people's actions, migrates out into the community. The conditions for this migration were set because Whirlpool actively encourages and models social responsibility and community involvement. Innovators are passionate about their craft and find uses for the tools that are meaningful and personal to them. What part of your job becomes a part of you? Innovation may be in a class by itself, taking root in people and changing their DNA.

What Dave Whitwam Started

Dave Whitwam is one of the world's great visionaries, but we doubt that even he fathoms the breadth and scope of what he unleashed in autumn 1999. Jeff Fettig has shaped innovation and moved it to new frontiers, but even his strength of leadership cannot require innovation from everyone unless people are emotionally attached. It is the people, the innovators, who are the stars. There are thousands of them at Whirlpool, those who buck convention, take risks, and work doggedly to launch unique products or find blue oceans where only a sea of red exists. They dare to go where the dragons are.

References

Andrew, J. P., and Sirkin, H. L., with Butman, J. *Payback—Reaping the Rewards of Innovation*. Boston: Boston Consulting Group, 2006.

Arthur Andersen. "What Makes Innovation Firms Different." *Businessline*, Aug. 5, 2004, p. 1.

Basadur, M., and Gelade, G. "The Role of Knowledge Management in the Innovation Process." *Creativity and Innovation Management*, Mar. 2006, *15*(1), 45.

Bass, E., and Bass, S. (Directors). *Why Man Creates*. Film. Santa Monica, Calif.: Pyramid Media, 1968.

Boeddrich, H.-J. "Ideas in the Workplace: A New Approach Towards Organizing the Fuzzy Front End of the Innovation Process." *Creativity and Innovation Management*, Dec. 2004, *13*(4), 274–285.

Boston Consulting Group. *Measuring Innovation*. (Senior Management Survey). Boston: Boston Consulting Group, 2006.

Brady, E. "Soul of a Champion: Athletes Share Common Competitive Thread." *USA Today*, Sept. 25, 2006. www.usatoday.com/sports/soac/2006-09-21-introduction-cover_x.htm.

Burt, R. "Structural Holes and Good Ideas." *American Journal of Sociology*, Sept. 2004, *110*(2), 349–400.

Campbell, J. *The Hero with a Thousand Faces*. Princeton, N.J.: Princeton University Press, 1969.

Christensen, C. Keynote address. World Innovation Forum, New York, June 6, 2007.

Collins, J. S., and Porras, J. I. "Building Your Company's Vision." *Harvard Business Review*, Sept.-Oct. 1996, pp. 65–77.

Csikszentmihalyi, M. *Good Business: Leadership Flow and the Making of Meaning*. New York: Viking, 2003.

De Cagna, J. [Posting to the Fast Company.com innovation blog]. Aug. 9, 2005. http://blog.fastcompany.com/archives/2005/08/09/inclusive_innovation.html#comments. Used with permission from Jeff De Cagna and FastCompany.com.

Drucker, P. F. "The Discipline of Innovation." *Harvard Business Review*, Aug. 1, 2002. Reprint R0208F.

"Expanding the Innovation Horizon: The Global CEO Study." Somers, N.Y.: IBM Global Business Services, 2006.

Foley, J. "Center of Creativity." *InformationWeek*, Mar. 15, 2004. www. informationweek.com/news/showArticle.jhtml?articleID18312026.

Gallup. "Engaged Employees Inspire Company Innovation." http://gmj. gallup.com/content/24880/Gallup-Study-Engaged-Employees-Inspire-Company.aspx. (Accessed Nov. 27, 2007)

Getz, I., and Robinson, A. G. "Innovate or Die: Is That a Fact?" *Creativity and Innovation Management*, Sept. 2003, *12*(3), 130–136.

Gilder, G. *The Spirit of Enterprise*. New York: Simon & Schuster, 1984.

Hamel, G. *The Future of Management*. Boston: Harvard Business School Press, 2007.

Hammer, M. "Deep Change: How Operational Innovation Can Transform Your Company." *Harvard Business Review*, Apr. 1, 2004. Reprint R0404E.

Hansen, M. T., and Birkinshaw, J. "The Innovation Value Chain." *Harvard Business Review*, June 1, 2007. Reprint R0706J.

Harkema, S. "A Complex Adaptive Perspective on Learning Within Innovation Projects." *The Learning Organization: An International Journal*, 2003, *10*(6), 340–346.

Hesselbein, F. "The Key to Cultural Transformation." *Leader to Leader*, Spring 1999, no. 12, p. 6.

Hindo, B. "At 3M, a Struggle Between Efficiency and Creativity." *BusinessWeek*, June 11, 2007. www.businessweek.com/magazine/content/07_24/b4038406.htm.

Huston, L., and Sakkab, N. "Connect and Develop: Inside Procter & Gamble's New Model for Innovation." *Harvard Business Review*, Mar. 1, 2006. Reprint R0603C.

Kanter, R. M. "How Cosmopolitan Leaders Inspire Confidence." *Leader to Leader*, Summer 2006, no. 41, p. 56.

Kaplan, R. S., and Norton, D. P. "The Balanced Scorecard: Measures That Drive Performance." *Harvard Business Review*, July 1, 2005. Reprint R0507Q.

Kim, W., and Mauborgne, R. "Blue Ocean Strategy, from Theory to Practice." *California Management Review*, Spring 2005, *47*(3), 105–121.

Lawrence, G. "Social Dreaming and Sustained Thinking." *Human Relations*, May 2003, *56*(9), 609–629.

Leib, S. "Principles of Adult Learning." Fall 1991. http://honolulu.hawaii. edu/intranet/committees/FacDevCom/guidebk/teachtip/adults-2.htm.

Linder, J. "Does Innovation Drive Profitable Growth? New Metrics for a Compete Picture." *Journal of Business Strategy*, 2006, *27*(5), 38–44.

Mariello, A. "The Five Stages of Successful Innovation." *MIT Sloan Management Review*, Spring 2007, pp. 8–9.

Morong, C. "The Creative-Destroyers: Are Entrepreneurs Mythological Heroes?" Paper presented at the annual conference of the Western Economic Association, San Francisco, July 1992.

Morong, C. "Mythology, Joseph Campbell, and the Socioeconomic Conflict." *Journal of Socioeconomics*, Winter 1994, *23*(4).

Muller, A., Välikangas, L., and Merlyn, P. "Metrics for Innovation: Guidelines for Developing a Customized Suite of Innovation Metrics." *Strategy and Leadership*, 2005, *33*(1), 35–45.

Parnaby, P., and Sacco, V. "Fame and Strain: The Contributions of Mertonian Deviance Theory to an Understanding of the Relationship Between Celebrity and Deviant Behavior." *Deviant Behavior*, 2004, *25*, 1–24.

Prahalad, C. K. "The Innovation Sandbox." *Strategy + Business*, Aug. 2006. www.strategy-business.com/press/freearticle/06306.

Schneider, P. "Importance of User Contact on the Increase." *Espertise*, July 2006. http://multimedia.mmm.com/mws/mediawebserver.dyn?6666660Zjcf6lVs6EVs66SfVXCOrrrrQ-.

Schredl, M., and Erlacher, D. "Self-Reported Effects on Dreams on Waking-Life Creativity: An Empirical Study." *Journal of Psychology*, 2007, *12*(1), 35–46.

Schulman, P. "Heroes, Organizations and High Reliability." *Journal of Contingencies and Crisis Management*, June 1996, *4*(2), 72–82.

Secretan, L. "Leadership: Learning How to Dream Again." *Journal of Financial Planning*, Dec. 2006, pp. 81–82.

"The Seed of Apple's Innovation." *BusinessWeek*, Oct. 12, 2004. http://businessweek.com/bwdaily/dnflash/oct2004/nf20041012_4018_db083.htm.

Sims, G. *Individuals Who Dream: Solutions for Management.* Unpublished dissertation, Capella University, Jan. 2000.

Snyder, N., and Duarte, D. *Strategic Innovation: Embedding Innovation as a Core Competency in Your Organization.* San Francisco: Jossey-Bass, 2003.

Taking Children Seriously. "Creativity." *TCS Glossary.* www.takingchil—drenseriously.com/node/50. 2008.

"Towers Perrin Study Finds Significant 'Engagement Gap' Among Global Workforce." *Business Wire*, Oct. 22, 2007. www.pr-inside.com/towers-perrin-study-finds-significant-engagement-r258363.htm.

Vera, D., and Crossan, M. "Strategic Leadership and Organization Learning." *Academy of Management Review*, Apr. 2004, *29*(2), 222–240.

Welbourne, T. M. "Employee Engagement: Beyond the Fad and into the Executive Suite." *Leader to Leader*, Spring 2007, no. 44, pp. 203–224.

Zander, R., and Zander, B. *Leadership: An Art of Possibility.* Videotape. Chicago: Groh Productions, Feb. 2001.

Acknowledgments

One of the premises of embedded innovation is that there are no lone innovators; it takes teams of people to innovate. The same is true for the production of *Unleashing Innovation*. I am indebted to many people who helped and supported me as Deb and I wrote this book. First my thanks go to Deb Duarte, my coauthor and friend, who helped with sections of the book and with the overall concept of how the book should be structured.

To Neal Maillet, who started this by calling me one day and challenging me to write a book that is different, and true to the amazing story of innovation at Whirlpool. Next, to the remarkable team at Jossey-Bass. I owe a great deal to Byron Schneider for his oversight and leadership and for his energy and positive influence in my work, and to Rebecca Browning, who coached and guided my work and gave me enormous support and help at every turn. Also my great appreciation to Susan Williams for my long-term partnership with Jossey-Bass. I count my blessings that I was introduced to Alan Shrader. The book would not have been possible without his amazing power to grasp the Whirlpool business case and then massage the manuscript into a story with a beginning, middle, and end that was easy to follow. I am both humbled by his skills and happy to find a colleague who shares my work ethic and deadline focus, but with a Zen sanity. It was also my pleasure to collaborate with Andrea Flint, my production editor, who worked out each and every flaw, adding the final shine to the manuscript.

I continue to be indebted to three visionary leaders who started it all. First to David R. Whitwam, who created the bold vision and held the critics at bay while he built innovation at Whirlpool. His ability to create new spaces with confidence and foresight made all of this possible. To Jeff Fettig, who guided innovation and shaped it into one of the key economic engines of Whirlpool. And to Gary Hamel, who challenged the business world before any of us were thinking about innovation or core competency and who continues to help Whirlpool embed innovation.

I have been fortunate to work with many wonderful professionals at Whirlpool who led and continue to lead innovation. Mike Todman has been a staunch advocate for innovation and has the uncanny ability to point out innovation foibles and apply his leadership to keep innovation on track. Also my thanks to Marc Bitzer, who always offered encouragement and innovation leadership. The facilitators of innovation include Giuseppe Geneletti, Barbara Rand, Pam Rogers, Rainer Blesch, Ricardo Acosta, and Warwick Stirling, who all were in a lead innovation role at Whirlpool, each contributing significantly to its success. Special thanks to Sean Lindy, who played such a critical role in hardwiring innovation into the management systems for the executive committee. I also have a world-class team of people who help Whirlpool develop leadership and strategic capabilities, including Tammy Patrick and Kim Thompson, who played such a critical role in migrating the innovation process to leadership decisions. Monica Brunkel, Silvia Baldin, and especially Donna Paskin also helped in countless ways to get the book from concept to manuscript.

Whirlpool continues to have a strong relationship with Strategos. I am particularly indebted to David Crosswhite, who was with Whirlpool from the beginning, and Peter Skarzynski, who continues to work with me on many innovation fronts.

I have been fortunate to work through my learning of innovation with the help of my students at Notre Dame and the

University of Chicago. I am especially indebted to Harry Davis of the University of Chicago for his wise counsel and support at every turn. Also to Holly Raider, who played a key role in helping leaders apply innovation to decision making, and to Stacey Kole of the GSB, who continues to support my efforts to learn and teach about innovation. I also add Mike Tobin to my list of colleagues who gave me support and insights as I worked through the book.

I set up a Whirlpool editorial board to make sure that my writing was true to the story and credible to the people of Whirlpool. They had the unenviable task of reading the first draft. I am forever indebted to Mike Thieneman for his insight, guidance, and leadership as the executive committee sponsor, and to Andrew Batson, JD Rapp, and Barbara Rand, among others already mentioned.

I also had great assistance from the Whirlpool legal department: Dan Hopp, Bob Kenegy, and Michel Rose, who toiled over the manuscript and offered sage counsel.

I am inspired by the I-mentors of Whirlpool and all the people who allowed me to interview them for this book, including the Centralpark team, and I am particularly grateful to Hank Marcy for all his contributions to the book and to innovation at Whirlpool. I count myself fortunate to work with so many outstanding professionals from Whirlpool, past and present.

I am blessed to have such a wonderful family and set of friends to keep me going and not let me take things too seriously. To Robert, who proofed and critiqued early drafts when no one wanted to read them and who constantly supports me and my endeavors, and to my sisters and their families for their love and support at every step. Also to my yoga teacher, Maria Rosner, who helped me de-stress through yoga and introduced me to the soundtrack of *The Hours*, which I used every time I sat down to write.

About the Authors

Nancy Tennant Snyder is currently the corporate vice president for leadership and strategic competencies for Whirlpool Corporation, reporting to the chairman and CEO, Jeff M. Fettig. In this capacity, she is responsible for creating and implementing enterprise strategies that facilitate innovation leadership, leveraged learning, and competitive knowledge. She heads the David R. Whitwam Centre for Leadership and Lifelong Learning, Whirlpool's corporate university. She is a faculty member of the University of Chicago Graduate School of Business, teaching strategy, innovation, and organization change, and most recently of the University of Notre Dame Business School. She is one of the world's leading thinkers and practitioners in transforming large business environments to achieve innovation from everyone and everywhere. In 2006, *BusinessWeek* named Snyder one of the twenty-five Innovation Champions (IN25) in the world.

Snyder holds a doctorate in organizational behavior from George Washington University. She is a board member of the First Tee of Benton Harbor, a nonprofit organization that offers character development and life skills to youth at risk through golf. Snyder can be reached through Whirlpool at Nancy_T_Snyder@whirlpool.com or through the Whirlpool Web site (www.whirlpoolcorp.com).

Deborah L. Duarte is an expert in the areas of innovation strategy, leadership and executive development, organizational design, project leadership, virtual teaming, and executive coaching. She consults in these areas with a number of private and public organizations, including Whirlpool, the National Aeronautics and Space Administration, Colgate Palmolive, ExxonMobil, Discovery Communications, Cemex, Merrill Lynch, Citi, General Dynamics, and others. Deborah is an adjunct faculty member at George Washington University and teaches courses in organizational diagnosis, leadership, organizational learning, and research methods. Duarte holds a doctorate in organization and human resource development from the George Washington University. She is a frequent presenter at conferences and workshops.

Snyder and Duarte have coauthored two best-selling books: *Mastering Virtual Teams* and *Strategic Innovation*, both published by Jossey-Bass.

Index